Password authentication for web and mobile apps

Dmitry Chestnykh

Version v1.0.5

2020-08-06

Contents

Introduction

How to authenticate users? It seems like we figured it out a long time ago. Millions of websites and apps ask you to enter your username and password to let you in. There are hundreds of frameworks that you can plug into your app to get it working. How hard can it be?

Still, app developers often get it wrong. Developers of authentication frameworks sometimes get it wrong. There doesn't seem to be an end to strange decisions and mistakes made by us, developers. Users still can't revoke access from devices they lose or that get stolen. They still suffer from usability quirks. They still struggle with arbitrary limits on how their passwords should look. They still have their passwords leaked and cracked.

This book is an attempt to put an end to all of this. You will find detailed instructions on how to implement your own secure password-based authentication system with multi-factor authentication that allows resetting and changing passwords, listing and revoking sessions, safely changing usernames and email addresses.

The book is written for every developer: even if you don't deal with authentication directly, it will be useful to learn how it works. If you're a developer of an authentication framework, you will learn how to make it secure and to avoid common mistakes.

There isn't much sample code. Instead, the concepts and algorithms are explained in English, with references to third-party libraries where appropriate.

This book will not teach you how to implement authentication with third-party services using OAuth, SAML or the newest WebAuthn (except when used as a second factor): these deserve their own separate books. First, we need to get the basics right.

Basics

Cryptography

Cryptography is essential for any application today. However, there is a tendency to overuse it when a simple solution without any cryptography would work better and be more secure.

Apart from the transport security, TLS, user authentication with passwords requires only two cryptographic things: a cryptographically secure random number generator and a password hashing function. While other primitives, such as cryptographic hash functions, message authentication codes and authenticated encryption, will be discussed in this book, they are absolutely not required. In fact, using them without careful design and implementation can make your app less secure, due to architectural or implementation errors. You cannot just sprinkle some crypto on your code to make it more secure. The good old programmer's wisdom — *the number of bugs grows with the number of lines of code* — is even more powerful when you add cryptography.

I said that you need two things, but the first one — the secure random number generator — is already provided by your operating system and your programming language. Generating quality randomness is vital for security and is discussed in the Randomness section.

The only thing you definitely need to add is a password hashing function. Hashing passwords is the only way we know how to keep user accounts secure even if the passwords database is leaked. See the Password hashing section.

Cryptography is fascinating, and once you learn about it, you want to use it to solve every problem. Fight this temptation. My guess is that most software in the world that uses cryptography (by the number of apps, not the number of installations) uses it insecurely. It's only partially a fault of the programmers who wrote those systems, it's also a fault of cryptographers (who don't think how their inventions will be used in the real world), of developers of programming languages and libraries (who insist on insecure defaults and primitives and don't document them properly), and, of course, of many people without the domain-specific knowledge who answer questions on StackOverflow, putting incorrect information to the top of search results.

If you find a solution for your problem on the Internet, and it uses cryptography, most likely there is an easier way to do it without any crypto.

Remember: if you have a choice of using fancy cryptography versus a plain old database, always choose the latter.

Randomness

We deal with random bytes a lot: use them for various identifiers, secret keys, CSRF tokens, session verifiers, etc. Randomness plays one of the most important parts in making our systems secure. Thus, we need good, secure randomness. What are its properties?

- It is unpredictable. Nobody can guess what the next bit will be, even if they've seen all previous bits; and nobody can guess previous bits, even if they see the future bits. (That is, the chance of guessing such a bit is not greater than random, 50%.)

- It has a uniform distribution.

Your server's operating system can generate such randomness. It uses a combination of various events collected from the system (timings from devices, such as hard drives and network cards) and a hardware random bit generator built into the CPU, and then mixes the bits using cryptography to ensure they are uniform. There is rarely a need to use external generators or install some tricky daemons to feed entropy into the system.

Most programming languages come with functions to generate cryptographically secure randomness. However, they also have math libraries with *insecure* random number generators, which are good enough for math and statistical problems, but when used for the cases mentioned above, they make applications vulnerable to trivial attacks. Never use such generators where a secure generator is needed. Here are some examples.

Insecure generators, do not use:

- JavaScript, Node.js: don't use `Math.random`.

- Go: don't use functions from `math/rand` package.

- Python: don't use `random` module.

- Ruby: don't use `Random` class.

- PHP: don't use `mt_rand` or `rand`.

- Java: don't use any of the millions of `random` or `Random` things.

Again, do *not* use the generators listed above. Additionally, make sure that you do not have any third-party dependencies that use them for things that require cryptographically secure randomness. For example, it is common to find UUIDv4 generators that use those, making unique identifiers not so unique.

Secure random generators that you should use:

- JavaScript (web browsers): use `window.crypto.getRandomValues`.

- JavaScript (Node.JS): use `crypto.randomBytes`.

- Go: use `crypto/rand` package.

- Python: use `secrets` standard module in 3.6+ or `os.urandom` in older versions.

- Ruby: use `securerandom` standard module.

- PHP: use `random_bytes` in 7+ or `openssl_random_pseudo_bytes` in older versions.

- Java: use `java.security.SecureRandom` class.

On Unix-like systems, you can get randomness by reading /dev/urandom device (if you do so, don't forget to handle *all* error cases and short reads). This is handy when, for example, you want to get some random bytes in the terminal. The following command will get 32 random bytes and encode them in Base64:

```
$ head -c32 /dev/urandom | base64

wD6NCcfQ0GOKlwZLyVH/ZqoULZdjU1l/CQwa8cyVc9Q=
```

(on Linux you can use `openssl base64` instead of `base64`)

Secure randomness is good, but for the result to be really secure, you need enough of it. As a rule of thumb, you shouldn't use fewer than 16 bytes (which is 128 bits of entropy[1]) for keys, tokens or identifiers. To make it clear: these are "full" bytes (0-255), not ASCII characters. Consider the example above: we got 32 bytes from the system, and then encoded them with Base64 into a 44-byte string. The result still contains *32 bytes of entropy*, not 44, because the alphabet has 64 items, not 256.

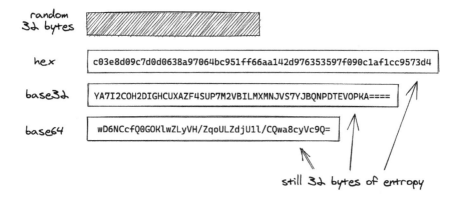

Regardless of how you encode the initial entropy, the result will never contain more of it: you can't get 256 bits of entropy from 128

bits, even if you hash them with SHA-512: the output will be 512 bits, but it will still contain 128 bits of entropy.

Modulo bias

Usually, we don't deal with bytes directly: we want random identifiers, random strings, etc. so we need to encode bytes into appropriate formats. With hex, Base32, and Base64 it is easy: we generate random bytes and then encode them. However, sometimes we want strings that contain only characters, or only numbers. That's when people make the most common mistake: they introduce modulo bias. It's called *modulo* bias because you get a number from a randomness generator and then use the modulo operation to fit it into the required range.

Here's an example in Node.js:

```
n = crypto.randomBytes(1)[0] % 64
```

You get one byte (a number in the range from 0 to 255) and then take modulo 64 to get the number in the range from 0 to 64 from it. This example doesn't have modulo bias, because the modulo is a power of two. However, if you want numbers in the range from 0 to 10, and you do:

```
n = crypto.randomBytes(1)[0] % 10 // incorrect!
```

your result will not be uniformly distributed from 0 to 10 — some numbers will be more likely to appear in the result than others.

You can check this by repeating the operation thousands of times and counting how often each number appeared. This is modulo bias — your result is biased for particular numbers because they appear with higher probability than others. The fact that your result is not uniform in rare cases can lead to a complete break of the system, and in most cases provides an advantage to the attacker (the search space is reduced). I have seen this mistake in password generators, token generators, and other apps.

If you need a random string containing only lower case English letters, you will take random numbers modulo 26. Since 26 is not a power of two, you will need to avoid modulo bias. You can do this by taking the nearest modulo that is a power of two that is greater than or equal to the modulo you want to take (for English letters, it is 32), and then rejecting results that are greater than your modulo (anything greater than 26) and generating the next random number until you get the one that's less than it.

To summarize: make sure your random strings or numbers don't have modulo bias and inspect third-party dependencies for this issue.

Here are some packages to generate random strings safely:

- Go: `github.com/dchest/uniuri`

- JavaScript: `@stablelib/random`

- Python: `secrets` standard module

- Ruby: `SecureRandom` has `alphanumeric`, `uuid`, `hex`, and `base64` methods

- Java: use nextInt() on SecureRandom to generate a uniform number to select an alphabet character. Here's an example: https://github.com/keycloak/keycloak/blob/ b478472b3578b8980d7b5f1642e91e75d1e78d16/common/src/ main/java/org/keycloak/common/util/RandomString.java

UUID

UUID (also known as GUID) is a common format of globally unique identifiers. A UUID looks like this:

```
7968f9b3-51d1-4d03-bd1a-ed13913fe0a6
```

There are many versions of UUID that were developed during the dark times when people were not sure how to generate random numbers. There are UUIDs that use MD5 and SHA-1 hashes, current time in the galaxy far, far away, and the number of bread-crumbs left in a server room by sysadmins during the full moon. The only good version is v4, generated using a secure randomness generator.

UUIDs are encoded in a funny way that makes them easily recognizable: hex characters split with dashes. When decoded into the original bytes, they are 16 bytes long, however, they do not contain 128 bits of entropy — some bits are reserved for the version and other silly stuff. In short, this '4' you see in the third group is a version number and the other two or three bits are taken to indicate the "variant". Bleh. So, your UUIDv4 will contain 121 or 122 bits of randomness. While it's a few bits lower than my recommendation for the minimal length of random byte arrays, it's still fine — it is infeasible that someone generates the same UUIDv4 as you or guesses the one you generated. They are still globally unique and unpredictable.

Summary:

- Use only UUIDv4 (fourth version).
- Use a UUID generator that gets entropy from a secure randomness generator.

Some known-good packages for UUIDv4:

- JavaScript: `@stablelib/uuid`
- Go: `github.com/google/uuid` (use `uuid.New` or `uuid.NewRandom`)
- Python: built-in `uuid.uuid4`
- Ruby: `SecureRandom.uuid` from the built-in `securerandom` module
- PHP: see https://gist.github.com/dchest/ e77e705ef2c120c262b58a7a4893df61
- Java: `java.util.UUID.randomUUID`

If you don't need UUIDs for compatibility with other systems, such as databases that have the UUID type, but need globally unique unguessable identifiers, consider just generating 16 or 32 random bytes (secure random bytes, as described above) and encoding them in hex (this will result in a 32- or 64-character string).

Constant-time comparison

Usually, when comparing byte arrays or strings, each byte from one string is compared with the corresponding byte in another string; if they differ, the loop stops and the function returns *false*, otherwise, the process continues until the difference is found or the string ends. In most cases, the early return is good and makes comparison faster, however when such an early-return comparison is used for bytes that must be kept secret, it can make timing attacks possible: an attacker makes guesses, measuring time differences between them. After adjusting for the noise, the attacker can spot when the server takes more time for comparison than before, thus correctly guessing a byte.

To prevent this attack, constant-time comparison functions are used: they perform bitwise operations on each byte instead of comparing them and accumulate the result, which is then returned after each byte of the two arrays is processed. These functions are difficult to write correctly, so stick with the known-good implementations. Many languages have them built-in (especially, in HMAC libraries, since variable time comparison of HMAC often leads to vulnerabilities).

Here are some examples:

- Go: `crypto/subtle` package or `hmac.Equal`

- Python: `hmac.compare_digest`

- JavaScript (Node.js): `crypto.timingSafeEqual`

- JavaScript (browsers): `@stablelib/constant-time`

- Ruby on Rails: `fixed_length_secure_compare` in `ActiveSupport::SecurityUtils`

The timing problem arises not only when directly using a comparison function. Consider a database index: depending on the implementation, it also can have timing differences when the database engine looks up the string. This is why you should not use secret tokens or identifiers as database keys if the inability to guess them is the only thing that makes the system secure: when the database lookup is not constant-time and depends on the bytes of the lookup string, the attacker can perform a timing attack and discover existing keys.

To avoid this error, use split tokens: where one part is a lookup string and another part is a string that will be compared in constant time. See Sessions and Universal confirmation system for details.

CSRF protection

This book is not about general web app security, but it is important to mention that you should use cross-site request forgery (CSRF or XSRF) protection. Your web framework probably comes with one.

Many CSRF prevention methods bind tokens to user sessions.

When the user is not logged in, there's no session, so there is a possibility of a login CSRF attack. Refer to the *Robust Defenses for Cross-Site Request Forgery* paper by Barth, Jackson, and Mitchell for more details (https://www.adambarth.com/papers/2008/barth-jackson-mitchell-b.pdf).

Audit logging and reporting

Audit logging is required for discovering attacks and vulnerabilities. At a minimum, the following actions concerning user accounts should be logged:

- Successful and unsuccessful log in attempts.
- Changes to usernames and email addresses.
- Changes to passwords.
- Password reset attempts.
- Multi-factor authentication set ups and use attempts.

You should *not* log passwords, password hashes, the verification part of sessions or confirmation tokens, or secret keys (including two-factor authentication keys).

You may want to notify users about successful log in attempts and important changes to their account by email. This will help them discover account breaches and take measures early.

—

[1] Why 128 bits? Key search in 2^{128} space would require more energy than can be

produced on Earth. For 256 bits — probably the energy of the observable Universe. (This is for a classical computer. Quantum computers, if they ever happen in a usable form, will roughly halve it.) It doesn't have to be this exact number, of course: 122 bits, as in UUIDv4, are still infeasible to guess. There are more to the attacks than just key search: for instance, birthday paradox (https://en.wikipedia.org/wiki/Birthday_problem), which is relevant for collisions, but doesn't apply to all cases.

Users

Usernames vs email addresses

There are two common approaches to identifying users: with usernames or email addresses. Sometimes they are used interchangeably.

A username is a short string that the user remembers. It's an alias or a pseudonym that the user enters into the sign in form along with the password to log in to the app. Usernames should be case-insensitive (that is, *John* and *john* is the same username). In most cases, usernames are chosen by users, but sometimes they are derived from their name or randomly chosen by the system. We'll focus on the first case, since it's the hardest.

Other systems require users to enter their existing email address to log in. While the two methods may seem similar, there is a huge difference between the approaches: allowing users to create a username instead of authenticating them by email enables pseudonymity. Such pseudonymity is important for websites for which revealing that a user has an account can cause harm: for example, for dating or adult websites.

With email addresses it is infeasible to not reveal user existence. Even if you don't reveal it during the sign in, you will have to do so during registration: when an attacker tries to register an account in the system with the victim's email, they will receive an error saying that such user already exists. With usernames, if correctly implemented and having no other leaks, all the attacker learns is that a username is already taken, but unless it is obvious from the username itself, there is no association between the username and a person or their email address: *bond007* may be *james@sis.gov.uk* or *danielcraig@eon.co.uk*. A correctly implemented system with pseudonymity must not reveal the association between emails and usernames at all stages: during the registration (no "such email exists" errors), logging in (no ability to log in with the email address), password reset, or username reminder. The app must also not leak username-email association in its business logic, such as when sharing a document with other users.

Filtering usernames

An application that allows users to choose their username inevitably becomes a victim of users that create undesirable usernames. Poor application! *Sevious buvinesses* don't want such usernames in their systems, so they ask to disallow profanities in them. Also, people with malicious intentions will try to create official-looking usernames, such as "admin" or "postmaster" or your company name, to mislead other users and perform phishing attacks. You may want to disallow creating accounts with such usernames. For that, you'll need a list of bad usernames.

While it may sound fun, you don't want to spend your days remembering all the bad words you know. Believe it or not, somebody already did! There are many lists that you can use that are available on the Internet.

Here are some of them:

- https://github.com/chucknorris-io/swear-words

- https://github.com/words/cuss

Don't forget to add words specific to your app, such as your company name (if you don't want to have an account for it yourself, of course).

Filtering out usernames that contain bad words sounds easy, but remember that users are inventive. They will replace o's with zeros, use the Cyrillic or Greek alphabet for some letters, etc. The solution is to normalize usernames before checking the list.

For demonstration purposes, since I don't want this book to have any profanities, let's imagine that the word "president" is a profanity from the banned words list. Some variations of it are:

1. pReSiDenT (different letter case)

2. pres1dent ('i' replaced with '1')

3. president123

4. president ('e' is actually Cyrillic)

5. motherpresident

6. pre_sid_ent

The first defense is to disallow usernames with characters outside of ASCII letter range 'a' to 'z'. (You may allow some separators, such as '_'.) This will prevent creating usernames with similar looking letters from other alphabets and prevent all Unicode trickery attacks. This may not work for some non-English apps, so use your judgment. If you allow other alphabets, make sure to normalize usernames before checking against the ban list using a simple letter replacement table (Cyrillic 'e' → Latin 'e', etc.)

Next, convert the username to lowercase.

Then replace all numbers in the username with letters that look similar.

```
0 → o
1 → i
2 → z
3 → e
4 → a
5 → s
6 → b
7 → t
8 → b
9 → g
```

Notice though that while our case, i → 1, is covered by this rule, '1' (one) also looks like lowercase 'L', so this case will slip through our rules. One way to solve this is to run the normalization again later, with a different table, in which '1' is replaced with 'l'.

If you allow separators, remove them.

Let's check what happens after the above steps to our usernames:

1. pReSiDenT → president

2. pres1dent → president

3. president123 → presidentize

4. president → (rejected, Cyrillic 'e' is not in allowed characters)

5. motherpresident → motherpresident

6. pre_sid_ent → president

Check out the third word: when it went through our normalizer, digits got replaced with letters. To cover this case, you'd want another normalizer: the one which removes numbers. In the end, we'll have more than one normalized username, and we want to check each of them against the banned words list.

After normalizing, we have a choice of how to approach the banned words lookup.

One way is to loop through the whole ban list and find each banned word as a substring in each normalized username. This search is linear, but since the ban lists usually contain a thousand or so items and usernames are limited in length, it will be quite fast on modern computers. This algorithm will reliably find the banned word if it's a part of the username (such as "motherpresident"), however, its weakness is that it will produce a lot of false positives since some bad words are part of good words. French "Canal Plus" and Mr. Cumming won't be able to create accounts in your system.

Another way — that will give no false positives, but will not filter out multi-part bad words — is to search for each normalized username in the list of bad words. (If you allow separators, split the username at the separator character.) With this algorithm, you won't catch "motherpresident", but will not have to deal with false positives. This is my preferred way to filter out usernames. There are also some fuzzy search algorithms, but they also produce false positives.

Finally, if your algorithm decides that a username contains a banned word, return an error to the user and allow them to create a different username.

Validating email addresses

The only way for a web app to ensure that the email address entered by the user is correct is to send a confirmation link to this address and wait for it to be clicked. Email confirmation is described in the next section. However, before you send the email, you may want to pre-validate the address to avoid angering the internet tubes.

Email addresses as defined by RFC 5322 are incredibly complicated, mostly for legacy reasons. You may have seen the incredible Perl regular expression that can validate them at something like 99.99% success rate:

Wait, is it sideways? With regular expressions, we'll never know...
Source: http://www.ex-parrot.com/pdw/Mail-RFC822-Address.html

To be honest, you don't want this complexity. Almost nobody uses the email address format to their fullest, and if they do, they wouldn't be able to enter such an address into many other websites, and you probably don't want those eccentric people as your users. Who knows what else they can do to your system?! Instead, I recommend sticking to a simple regular expression that will validate 99.9% of addresses that exist in real world and sometimes let invalid addresses through. I use one that I stole from the WebKit browser engine which uses it to validate input fields with email type. If browsers can do it, you can do it.

Here's the regexp (written in JavaScript format):

```
[a-z0-9!#$%&'*+/=?^_`\{|}~.-]+@[a-z0-9-]+(.[a-z0-9-
]+)*$/gi
```

Nowadays domains can contain non-ASCII characters, for example, пример.испытание is a valid Cyrillic domain name. Email doesn't really work with such addresses, instead, users on this domain must use the Punicode variant of the address, for example `user@xn--e1afmkfd.xn-80akhbyknj4f`.

You can do more than validating the email address with regexp: you can check if the domain of the address has MX records with a DNS request. You don't want to do it if you send a confirmation email anyway, but I'll mention this just in case you want to quickly reject invalid addresses. Extract the domain part from the email address and issue a DNS request to the domain asking for its MX record. If you get the record, then this domain can accept emails. Of course, this doesn't guarantee that this server *will* accept them or that the user with the address exists.

Confirming email addresses

Email addresses should be confirmed to ensure they belong to the user. Failing to do so will annoy people who receive emails from your service, to which they didn't sign up, and will annoy your users who would wonder why they didn't receive emails from you or why they couldn't access their account or reset their password. This happens when users mistype their email address or when malicious users type somebody else's address.

There's an annoying person in this world, who thinks that my email address is hers and uses it to sign up for many services. I receive notifications about servicing her Kia, emails about how Domino's prepares her pizza and when it gets delivered. I also have a Starbucks card, thanks to her, which unfortunately I can't use because there's no Starbucks in my country. I potentially have full access to her accounts. (If you're wondering, yes, I notified some of those services, and some even replied back promising to review their security policies.) This happens because these services failed to confirm the email address before allowing the user account to become active. (Of course, with some systems I could still confirm "my" account when she created a Starbucks account with my email address, and take it over. This is prevented by requiring an active session or entering the password.)

More importantly, not confirming email addresses, when combined with other vulnerabilities, can help attackers steal accounts. This happened to Skype in 2012: they allowed adding email addresses to accounts without confirming them. I noticed this in August when I received an email from them thanking me for registering an account. But I already had an account, I didn't register a new one. After comparing the new account name with my email, I came to the conclusion that someone mistyped their email address, and registered an account on my address. I contacted Skype to tell them that this was a security issue, but they didn't fix it (It went something like this: "Why don't you verify emails?" — "Please understand that all of us here at Skype take our customers' privacy and confidentiality very seriously" — "Yeah, right...") I then created an account for Bill Gates and went on with my life. Later someone combined this with another vulnerability (which was also reported before), and was able to take over existing accounts by creating a new account, adding the existing account's email address to it (remember, there was no confirmation), and then triggering password reset which allowed them to select either of the accounts.

So, you should confirm the email address when a user creates an account. You should also perform confirmation when they change the email address.

There are two ways to implement it: make the account active only when the user confirms their email, or activate the account, but mark the email address as unconfirmed and disallow certain actions related to it, until it is confirmed.

If you use email addresses for logging in, consider the fact that malicious persons can create accounts for many email addresses that they do not own and cannot confirm. When the actual owner of the email address decides to create an account, they will be turned away, since the account for that email already exists in the system. One solution is to disable any use of the account until the email address is confirmed. If the account stays unconfirmed for a day or two, delete it.

On the server, the confirmation will work like this:

1. Generate a confirmation token — two 16-byte values, an identifier and a verifier — and combine them into a link that the user will click to verify their address.

2. Store the identifier (indexed for search) and a cryptographic hash of the verifier, and the user ID.

3. Send the link to the email address that is being verified.

When the user clicks on the link, the server splits the received token into the identifier and the verifier, looks up the record by the identifier, and, if found, compares (in constant time) the hash of the received verifier with the hash stored in the database. If the hashes are equal, it marks the email address as verified. This must be done in the authenticated state — that is, when the user who clicked the link has an active session (if not, redirect to the log in form or ask for the password). The authenticated state is needed so that only the user that created the account and knows the password for it can confirm the email address.

When changing the email address, you do not want to replace the existing one before the new one is verified: if the user mistypes their address, they could lose access to their account. So, when the user requests the email address change, send out the confirmation email as described above, and replace the old email with the new confirmed one only when confirmation succeeds. This can be generalized into a universal confirmation system.

Universal confirmation system

The confirmation system enables users to confirm certain actions out-of-band with a one-time use token.

The action type to be confirmed is stored on the server along with the information describing it. Here's a basic structure for confirmations table in the database:

- `confirmation_id` (primary key)

- `verifier_hash`

- `user_id`

- `created_at` (timestamp)

- `expires_at` (timestamp)

- `action_type`

- `details`

To initiate the action confirmation, the server creates a two-part token consisting of a confirmation identifier and a verifier, each containing 16 random bytes (the identifier can be a UUID, see the UUID section for details, or a MongoDB's ObjectId). The verifier is hashed with SHA-256 and stored as `verifier_hash` in the database[2]. The identifier and the verifier (the original 16-byte value, not the hash) are combined into the token, which is then provided to the user via a secondary channel, for example, sent by email. (Make sure the token is not revealed via the original channel — the app — otherwise, the confirmation act will be useless.)

To confirm the action, when the user provides the token, for example, by clicking on the link in the email that points to the URL containing the token, the server splits it into the two original parts: the identifier and the verifier. Then it looks up the record in the database by the identifier, and if found, it makes sure that the record is not expired by checking the expiration timestamp. Then the server computes the SHA-256 hash of the verifier extracted from the received token and compares this hash with `verifier_hash` stored in the database record. If the hashes are equal, it performs whatever action is described in the record with the details. For example, if the action type is *change_email*, it extracts the new email address from `details` and sets it as the confirmed email address of the user.

Consider email change. As discussed in the Confirming email addresses section, when a user changes their email address in the UI, we do not want to replace the email address in the user record immediately: instead, we should keep the previous address there until the user confirms the new address. Thus when the server receives a request to change the email, it performs the following steps. (In our example, the user changes email from *alice@example.com* to *fox@example.net*.)

1. Generate a confirmation identifier (16 random bytes or UUID) and a 16-byte verifier. For example, in hex encoding:

   ```
   confirmation_id: c4ed4a01478cbe2d93fb92996a6fa6f5
   verifier: 80a498a2a98ce5b31299ec05f200c77e
   ```

2. Hash the verifier with SHA-256:

   ```
   verifier_hash = SHA-256(verifier)
   ```

for our example, this will be:

```
verifier_hash:
11d1af2c637929b9305140c6f833e97a3d520123904127de961633
8cdba32bd9
```

3. Store `confirmation_id`, `verifier_hash` and the following additional information in the database:

```
action_type: "email_change"
details: {
    old: "alice@example.com",
    new: "fox@example.com"
}
created_at: current timestamp
expires_at: current timestamp plus 12 hours
```

4. Combine `confirmation_id` and `verifier` (not `verifier_hash`!) into a single string:

```
c4ed4a01478cbe2d93fb92996a6fa6f5.80a498a2a98ce5b31299e
c05f200c77e
```

and send it to the user by email, for example:

```
You have requested email change for account X. Click
on this link to confirm this email address:

https://example.com/?confirm=c4ed4a01…

If you didn't request the email change, do not click
on the link.
```

When the user clicks on the link:

1. Split the received token into two parts:

   ```
   confirmation_id: c4ed4a01478cbe2d93fb92996a6fa6f5
   verifier: 80a498a2a98ce5b31299ec05f200c77e
   ```

2. Lookup the record in the database for `confirmation_id`. If not found, return an error indicating that the confirmation token is wrong.

3. Check that `expires_at` from the database record is in the future from the current time. If not, return an error indicating that the token is expired.

4. Calculate SHA-256 of the verifier and compare it with the `verifier_hash` from the database record. If they don't match, return the same error as in step 1.

5. If you use the same URL for all actions, figure out what action needs to be performed by looking at `action_type` field in the database record. In our case, it's *email_change,* so perform the email change algorithm at step 6.

6. Extract confirmation action details from the database record. In our case, it contains "old" — email address to change from, and "new" — email address to change to. First, ensure that the user's record has the old address (this prevents race conditions), and if not, cancel the action. Otherwise, replace the email address in the user record with the new one. That's it.

After every action that returns an error (except for the first one) and after completing the final step, remove the record from the confirmations table. You also want to periodically remove expired records (the ones that have expires_at field in the past from the current time) to avoid overfilling the database. Some databases can be configured to expire items automatically, for others you'll need to perform garbage collection programmatically at regular intervals.

In the example we used 12 hours as the expiration time for the email change confirmation. This seems reasonable to me, but you can adjust it to your requirements. Remember that users may not have access to their email account immediately at the time when they initiate the change.

If you want to use this system for password resets, do not store the old password hash in the confirmations record — instead, store the old salt only, or just allow non-transactional updates to passwords.

Changing usernames

If your app uses usernames, you may want to allow users to change them. It's not as simple as updating the database record: carefully consider all the consequences. For example, if your app involves sharing or public access, how would other users who shared information with that user notice the change in the username? What if you tell someone to send important documents to *mansur123*, but Mansur changed the username, and the documents end up going to the void or, worse, to someone who took the old username?

Ideally, don't release old usernames to other users (but allow the user who changed it to go back to the old one).

This may present a problem though: squatters can take all the good usernames. Make sure to rate-limit registrations and the number of times your users can change usernames within a certain period (for example, no more than twice per year).

If some resources are accessed by username, consider redirecting from the old username to the new one.

Changing email addresses

Changing email addresses for users is more complicated than simply updating the record in the database.

You want to confirm the new email address by sending a token to it. The email is confirmed when the user clicks on the link that contains the token. Before this happens, though, you do not want to actually change the current email address. The reasoning for this is that the user may have mistyped the address, thinking that they changed it to the correct one, but when they try to log in the next time, they would type the correct address, while your database has the mistyped one, so they will no longer be able to log in or reset their password.

You will need the following transactional system:

1. Remember the current and the new email address.

2. Send the confirmation email to the new address.

3. When confirmed, check that the current address for the user record is the one you remembered for this transaction. If it is, replace it with the new address. If it's not, abort the change.

The part about remembering the current address is important to prevent a race condition: the user may have changed the address twice, for example:

- current address: *a@example.com*

- new address: *b@example.com*

- oops, no, actually, the new address is: *c@example.com*

Now, imagine that all three addresses belong to the user. They will receive two confirmation messages: first to confirm *b@example.com*, and then *c@example.com*. The user really wants to change it to *c@example.com*, and so clicks the last link. However, later they find the first confirmation email and also click a link on it. If your system keeps transactions like this, tracking *from → to* changes:

a@example.com → b@example.com

a@example.com → c@example.com

since the user already changed the current address to *c*, but the transaction was from *a* to *b*, it will not act on that last confirmation, which prevents the user's mistake.

For the complete algorithm on changing email addresses with confirmations, see Universal confirmation system.

The security of most systems depends on the email address. It is important to prevent attackers, who gain temporary access to the user's session, from changing it. To do so, your email change form (or access to it) should require entering the current password for the change to proceed.

Requiring re-authentication

Important actions with user accounts, such as changing the password, must require the current password to perform. This is needed to prevent an attacker that gets temporary access to the user's session, such as by using their computer when they leave it unattended, from changing the user's password or other information.

Changing the email address is also an important action: since most systems can initiate the password reset by email, if someone were to replace the user's email to the email under their control by gaining temporary access to the user's session, they could gain the full permanent access to the account by resetting the password.

Unicode issues

Unicode is a vast standard and has many interesting features that affect the security of the system. We already discussed how multiple users can have similar-looking usernames if you don't limit the alphabet by replacing Latin characters with characters from other alphabets that look the same. Here are some other things that you should be careful with at every part of the system that uses text, including email addresses.

Lowercase to uppercase transforms can be lossy. For example, there is no uppercase German letter 'ß' — the uppercase representation of it is 'SS' (to be precise, it was added to Unicode 5.1, but is rarely used). Thus, when you transform it to uppercase, and back to lowercase, you will get 'ss'. Here's a JavaScript example:

```
> "straße".toUpperCase().toLowerCase()
"strasse"
```

If you normalize data and then compare the result, make sure you consider this. This Unicode quirk allowed stealing accounts on GitHub: they normalized email addresses in one part of the system, however, sent messages to non-normalized addresses. You could have registered an account with Turkish lowercase 'ı' — *mıke@example.com* — then trigger the password reset, and it would send the email to that address, but for the account registered under the normalized address which is *mike@example.com* with Latin 'i'[3].

There are invisible codes that change text direction. This was used in the Telegram attack that distributed malware in 2018[4]: users received a message with an attachment that looked like an innocent PNG image, such as `photo_high_resj.png`, however, the actual file name was `photo_high_re` followed by the text direction change code U+202E followed by `gnp.js`. The actual file was a JavaScript

script! When users clicked on it, they thought they opened an image, but instead, they launched a malicious script. To protect against this attack, you can sanitize the text, removing text direction codes (but this may break right-to-left languages), or display text in a way that can't be faked. A file extension plays a vital part in recognizing the file type, so instead of displaying the filename as provided by the uploader, you can split the extension from it and display it separately. In browsers, text direction change won't affect the text outside of div or span tags, so it can be:

```
<span class="filename">photo_high_re[U+202E]gnp</span>
<span class="file-ext">.js</span>
```

—

[2] Storing the hash instead of the verifier protects against attackers confirming actions if the database is leaked.

[3] Hacking GitHub with Unicode's dotless 'i', https://eng.getwisdom.io/hacking-github-with-unicode-dotless-i/

[4] Zero-day vulnerability in Telegram, https://securelist.com/zero-day-vulnerability-in-telegram/83800/

Passwords

Password quality control

People are really bad at creating passwords. Those who don't use a password manager will likely create simple passwords that are easy to guess. While we can't solve this problem completely, we can at least enforce some standards for passwords to help users create safer ones.

The first line of defense against bad passwords is enforcing minimum length. Require at least 10 characters.

Next, for those passwords that satisfy the minimum length, use an algorithm that catches passwords that are too simple. While none of the password checking frameworks would guarantee that they'll reject all easy to guess passwords, they are very good for most of them.

My favorite library for checking password quality is *passwdqc*. Not only can it reject passwords that don't fit the given requirements based on the characters it contains, but it can also detect whether the password is a passphrase — a sequence of words — and act accordingly (passphrases have different measures for quality). It also can figure out if the password contains the elements of the username or other information about the account. Passwdqc catches more than 96% of the fourteen million leaked passwords from RockYou, which is a pretty good result considering it doesn't contain the database of those passwords: it's all enforced by a 4096-word list and clever rules.

Unfortunately, there is a limited variety of implementations of passwdqc — there is a C program (with Go, PHP, and Perl bindings) and a JavaScript port of a not-so-great quality. You can get them at https://www.openwall.com/passwdqc/.

The next best library, cryptically called *zxcvbn* from Dropbox, is easier to use and has been ported to many programming languages. It is larger, mostly because it contains a huge dictionary of words. You can get it from https://github.com/dropbox/zxcvbn.

You can perform the password quality check either on the client side or on the server. The client-side check is better from the usability point of view since the result can be viewed by the user immediately as they type their password.

There are third-party online services that can check passwords against the leaked databases. I don't recommend using them: first of all, you would be leaking some information about your user's password to them, secondly, you will have a huge single point of failure for registrations that will not depend on you, and finally, the libraries listed above already catch most of such leaked passwords. The diminishing returns you're getting from the services are not worth it. (You can, of course, implement your own using a publically available database of leaked passwords.)

Characters and emoji in passwords

What characters should be allowed in the password? In the ideal world, the best thing would be to not care about the characters at all, convert everything to UTF-8 bytes and accept all of them... but the computing world is not perfect. Two different systems can represent the same character differently. Do **é** and **é** look different to you? They look exactly the same, but they are different characters: the first one is U+00E9 LATIN SMALL LETTER E WITH ACUTE, the second one is U+0065 LATIN SMALL LETTER E (the normal 'e') followed by U+0301 COMBINING ACUTE ACCENT. If your user entered the first in one operating system, but then switched to a different one, which used the second representation when typing, then, if we just used password bytes directly, they wouldn't be able to log in.

You can play with encodings in your browser's developer console:

```
> "\u00e9"
"é"

> "\u0065\u0301"
"é"

> new TextEncoder().encode("\u00e9")
Uint8Array [195, 169]

> new TextEncoder().encode("\u0065\u0301")
Uint8Array [101, 204, 129]
```

NIST recommends[5] to normalize passwords using NFKC ("Normalization Form Compatibility Composition") or NFKD ("Normalization Form Compatibility Decomposition") normalizations[6] from the Unicode standard. Normalization turns different code points with the same meaning into an equal code point sequence. In our example, it will turn "e" combined with the acute accent into the "Latin small letter e with acute":

```
> "\u00e9".normalize("NFKC")
"é"

> "\u0065\u0301".normalize("NFKC")
"é"

> "\u0065\u0301".normalize("NFKC") ===
"\u00e9".normalize("NFKC")
true

> new TextEncoder().encode("\u00e9".normalize("NFKC"))
Uint8Array [195, 169]

> new
TextEncoder().encode("\u0065\u0301".normalize("NFKC"))
Uint8Array [195, 169]
```

As you can see, after normalization and encoding in UTF-8, both characters are the same.

OK, we figured out that we should normalize passwords, but should we allow emoji? Emoji are even worse than different representations of alphabet characters: they are constantly changing, their representations can vary greatly, their code points are sometimes reused, there are vendor-specific emoji... One of my favorite Twitter accounts, *@FakeUnicode*, has a great thread about emoji in passwords; the recommendation is to warn users about them. You can read the thread here:

https://twitter.com/FakeUnicode/status/1192245294429130752

The "get off my lawn" side of me wants to ban emoji in passwords, but on the other hand, those who try to use them maybe deserve the consequences?

Password hashing

When it comes to storing passwords on the server, the most common mistakes are storing them in plaintext, encrypting them instead of hashing, or hashing them with a hash function not suited for passwords.

Storing passwords as-is, in plaintext, is unsafe. The security goal of password storage for a typical web app, apart from the primary function of letting users in, is to prevent revealing any information about passwords if the password database is leaked. Storing plaintext passwords, obviously, reveals them all.

Some developers try to solve this by encrypting passwords with a secret key. Encryption may protect passwords from SQL injection or a similar attack on storage, but since the key is needed for decryption, the application server should know it, and so will the attacker who gets access to the server.

Then, there is hashing. It's an overloaded term for a one-way conversion of variable-length strings into a short fixed-length string that made many developers believe that using any cryptographic hash function, such as SHA-512, to hash passwords will make them secure. What do we actually need from the password hashing function?

1. It should be one-way: if an attacker gains access to the hash result, it must not be possible for them to reverse it or to find the original input faster than a dictionary attack (trying many password guesses by hashing them and comparing the output with the target hash).

2. An attacker must not learn that different users have the same password, or that a single user had the same password at different times. Thus the hashing function must produce different results for identical inputs when needed. This is achieved by including randomness into the hash function via salt.

3. It must be difficult for an attacker to perform a dictionary attack on many passwords at a low cost. (Difficult as in requiring a lot of time, hardware, or money.) This is achieved by using a specialized function designed specifically for hashing passwords.

4. Different passwords must not hash to the same output at a high enough probability.

Password hashing functions take the following inputs:

- password

- salt

- cost

Password is the password bytes (encoded in UTF-8 by convention).

Salt is an array of random bytes (usually 16 or 32 bytes).

Cost is a configurable parameter that defines how much time or computer resources it takes to produce the output. It is different for different password hashing algorithms: some take a single number, others take more parameters. It is important to know exactly what the cost parameter for each hashing function is, how it defines the resources to consume and what are the safe ranges for it.

A hash function will produce the output — password hash — that the server will store along with the salt and the cost. The salt and the cost are not encrypted or hashed — they are stored as-is. To verify the password, the server fetches the hash, the salt, the cost, and then runs the password hashing function with the original salt, the cost, and the given password to produce the hash. If this hash is equal to the stored hash, the password is correct.

The common password hashing functions are:

- PBKDF2

- bcrypt

- scrypt (and yescrypt)

- Argon2

A rule of thumb for password hashing: use the fastest implementation of the slowest algorithm.

PBKDF2

PBKDF2 means "Password-Based Key Derivation Function version Two". It is popular mainly because it's been out there for a long time, it is demanded by various bureaucratic standards, and it is widely available for many programming languages. However, it is the weakest of the password hashing functions covered in this book. I'd prefer not to cover it at all, but some developers have no choice and will have to use it, so they should know its issues and how to work around them.

Without getting into the algorithm details, basically PBKDF2 works by running a generic cryptographic hash function in a fancy way over the salted input as many times as you tell it to with the cost parameter, which is called "rounds" or "iterations".

When reading about PBKDF2, you'll notice abbreviation monstrosities, such as PBKDF2-HMAC-SHA-256[7]. What do they mean? PBKDF2-based variants are described using the PBKDF2-*PRF* notation, where *PRF* (pseudorandom function) is usually HMAC (hash-based message authentication code), which is described as HMAC-*Hash*, where *Hash* is the hash function. Confused? Don't be: it all boils down to special modes to run the underlying hash function, and we don't need to know all the internal details, we just need to know what hash functions are safe to use. PKBDF2 is commonly[8] used with SHA-256 or SHA-512. If you're going to use it on a 64-bit machine, use SHA-512. Never use

PBKDF2 with SHA-3 (it is slow in software — your case, but very fast and tidy in hardware — the attacker's case). Tune the iterations parameter so that it takes at least 200 ms to produce output. If it results in less than half a million iterations, you have a slow machine or implementation — find a better one.

Since all of the work inside PBKDF2 is iterating a hash function, attackers can easily parallelize the computation and use GPUs or ASICs to compute hashes, while your server will use a generic CPU. This means that attackers have a great advantage over you — while you may compute a single hash in 100 ms, the attackers will compute millions of them. This is why any modern app should not use PBKDF2.

Another issue with PBKDF2 is that while it allows computing a hash of any length, if you request more bytes than the output size of the hash function, the algorithm will perform twice or more computations to produce it. For example, if you request 64 bytes from PBKDF2-HMAC-SHA-256 with a million rounds, it will take two million rounds to compute it. This may sound not so bad until you realize that the shorter output is the prefix of the longer one, so the attacker doesn't need to compute the whole hash — they can just compute the first 32 bytes, which would be more than enough to learn if the password they tried is the password that produced the hash. If you're going to use PBKDF2 (don't!), make sure to not request more bytes than the hash output size. In fact, for password-based server authentication, you absolutely don't need more than 32 bytes in any case (see the Hash length section for details).

Requesting fewer bytes than the hash output size will not speed up computation.

Finally, there is one more issue with PBKDF2 (if it's used with HMAC, which is almost always how it's used). To describe it, we'll need to look deeper into the internals. HMAC accepts two parameters: a secret key and data. PBKDF2 puts the password into the secret key input, and the salt into the data input. Internally, HMAC either uses the key directly (okay), or if it's longer than the block size of the hash function, it will first compress the key with the hash function and then use the result as the key. This is problematic.

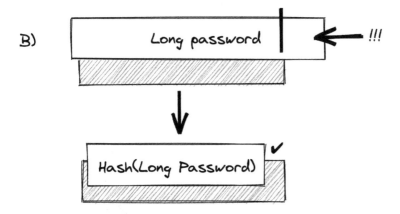

For instance, let's consider SHA-256 which has the block size of 64 bytes. If the key is longer than 64 bytes, the actual key that HMAC will use is SHA-256(key). Do you see the problem? Here's the trick: whether you input the original long key or SHA-256 hash of the original long key, you'll get the same output from HMAC! That's because the hash of the original long key will be shorter — 32 bytes for SHA-256 — than the hash block size, so HMAC will use it directly, but if you input the actual long key, it will use SHA-256 of that key. Which is the same thing! So, with PBKDF2-HMAC-SHA-256 any password longer than 64 bytes has another password that produces the same password hash. For most passwords, the second password would contain many unprintable characters, but with some effort, we can even calculate nice passwords that have a text-only hash doppelgänger. For example,

```
plnlrtfpijpuhqylxbgqiiyipieyxvfsavzgxbbcfusqkozwpngsyejql
mjsytrmd
```

and

```
eBkXQTfuBqp'cTcar&g*
```

hash to the same value with PBKDF2-HMAC-SHA-1[9]. To be fair, for most systems, this is not a problem. You need to know the long password in order to produce the second one (and it's infeasible to guess which long password hashes to the one you have). However, if the system assumes that only one password is valid, this issue breaks this assumption.

This issue can also bite you if your users reused their long password in some place where it was hashed with an unsalted hash, which is the underlying hash function that you use with PBKDF2, and the hash was leaked. This hash then can be directly used instead of the actual password to log in without even knowing the original password. In other words, if you use PBKDF2-HMAC-SHA-256(password), and someone leaked SHA-256(password), the attacker doesn't even have to know the password, they can just use the hash directly, if that password was longer than 64 bytes.

To summarize, `PBKDF2-HMAC-Hash(password)` is equal to `PBKDF2-HMAC-Hash(Hash(password))` for all cases where `length(password)` > `Hash block size`[10].

There is a trick to protect against this: it will be discussed in the scrypt and Prehashing for scrypt and bcrypt sections.

Anyway, don't use PBKDF2 unless you have very good reasons —
which are usually constraints outside of your sphere of influence.
No reputable cryptographer would recommend using PBKDF2
anymore. This is a legacy algorithm that should be considered
deprecated and not used in new systems.

PBKDF2 specification is available in RFC 8018: https://tools.ietf.
org/html/rfc8018.

bcrypt

Bcrypt is a password hashing function created by Niels Provos and
David Mazières in 1997 that takes a few kilobytes of memory and a
variable amount of computational power to compute the result.
Unlike PBKDF2 or scrypt, it is not a key derivation function: the
result of bcrypt is the hash encoded along with the salt and cost
parameter.

Bcrypt hashes look like this:

```
$2b$10$Mr6lCXuw0frE71i7MRNJR.qc4qjbmf6kIGMITklJ.ZVUiQVFuE
X3y
```

Bcrypt protects passwords better because it can't be computed on
GPU as efficiently as PBKDF2. Unlike scrypt or Argon2, the amount
of memory it takes for computation is fixed and cannot be
configured, so it is not as future-proof. Nevertheless, bcrypt is a
good option for hashing passwords, and it is easier to use than

PBKDF2 or scrypt. Twitter and GitHub use bcrypt to hash passwords. You should know about its quirks, though, and learn how to use it securely.

The cost parameter in bcrypt relates to the number of internal rounds. It is the power of two (cost 12 means 2^{12} rounds), thus incrementing this number will grow the computational cost exponentially.

Bcrypt uses 16-byte salts, which is good enough. Note that some old versions of some implementations had bugs, so make sure to use the latest version.

The downside of bcrypt is that the maximum password length it can hash is limited to 72 bytes, and most implementations just ignore anything beyond this. If you are going to use bcrypt, make sure to limit the password and report an error to the user if it is longer. Just ignoring everything beyond 72 bytes is dangerous: maybe the user's password is 72 a's followed some random characters. If you don't set the limit, the user may think that their password is secure, however, in reality, it only consists of 72 a's and all the good stuff after them is ignored.

This limitation can be worked around by prehashing the password with a cryptographic hash function, such as SHA-256, however, in this case, we'll end up building our own crypto, and, possibly, make serious mistakes.

Most bcrypt implementations accept NUL-terminated strings for a password. The incorrect implementation of prehashing used the result of the hash function directly as a password for bcrypt. Since the prehash could contain NUL bytes, it resulted in shorter or zero-length passwords (if the NUL byte was the first one). The correct implementation should encode the prehash in some UTF-8 -friendly format, such as hex or Base64. However, remember that when using SHA-512, which outputs 64 bytes, the bytes would be encoded as 128 hex characters, and so only the first 72 characters would be used as password — it's still good enough, but might be not what you expected. With SHA-256, 32 bytes give 64 hex bytes, which will be fully hashed with bcrypt.

In short, it's easier to limit passwords to 72 bytes than to play with cryptography. But make sure you're really counting bytes, not Unicode characters. For instance, in JavaScript, password.length will return the wrong result if you're expecting bytes when the password contains non-Latin characters or emoji. To count the bytes, encode the password into UTF-8 and count the length of the byte array.

To use bcrypt, you usually call bcrypt(password, cost) and save the result.

To verify a password, you call bcrypt_verify(hash, password).

To calculate the appropriate cost, run bcrypt on your server a few times at various costs and measure how long each run takes. Adjust the cost so that it takes at least 200 ms to compute the hash. If the cost is below 10, you're doing something wrong: this cost is too low for the current processing power.

The bcrypt specification is available at

https://www.usenix.org/legacy/events/usenix99/provos/provos_
html/node1.html

bcrypt implementations

- C: `crypt_blowfish` from Openwall (https://www.openwall.com/
  crypt/)

- Ruby: `bcrypt` gem

- Python: `passlib` package

- Go: `golang.org/x/crypto/bcrypt`

- Java: `jBCrypt`

scrypt

Scrypt is a password hashing function created by Colin Percival in
2009 that apart from doing CPU-consuming computations also uses
a specified amount of memory to do computations. Using more
memory increases the attacker's costs and makes parallel attacks
expensive. This is because having fast access to big amounts of
RAM makes it less advantageous for the attackers to build specialized devices versus running the attack on a generic computer — the
same hardware that you, as a defender, use to do the hashing.

Scrypt is a *sequential memory-hard function* which means that its
workload cannot be easily split into parts that use fewer amounts
of memory and run in parallel: all the memory that is set in the
cost parameters must be present and available to computation.

Scrypt accepts password bytes, salt bytes and three parameters: N, r, and p. It returns the requested amount of bytes as a hash (or a derived key). Like PBKDF2 and unlike bcrypt, scrypt output is a uniformly distributed pseudorandom value, thus to reproduce the result for verification, you should store the salt and the cost parameters. Don't use a single global configuration for N, r, p: store them in the database for each user. This will make it easy to upgrade the cost later.

- p is a parallelization parameter — basically, how many threads to use for computing the result.

- r is a block size parameter of the internal function — it is adjusted according to the internals of the CPU cache line size, and should be set to 8 for the currently available processors.

- N is a memory parameter — how much memory to consume for the computation. It must be a power of two. N is not alone in configuring RAM consumption: r and p also influence it.

The number of bytes of memory scrypt will use is roughly described with this formula:

```
memory = 128 * N * r * p
```

Let's say, you want your password hashing function to consume 256 mebibytes of RAM and use a single CPU core. To do this, set:

- $r = 8$ (don't change it to anything else as mentioned above)

- $p = 1$ (for the number of threads to run)

Then to calculate N:

```
N = memory / (128 * r * p)
```

In our case it will be:

```
N = (256 * 1024 * 1024) / (128 * 8 * 1) = 262144
```

(which is 2^{18})

Thus we call scrypt with the following arguments:

```
hash = scrypt(password, salt, N=262144, r=8, p=1)
```

If we fix r to 8 (which you should do), and use $p = 1$, an easy way to compute N would be:

```
N = memory / 1024
```

If we want to use two threads for computation, we set p to 2, but in this case each thread will use 256 MiB, so the total amount of RAM it will take is 512 MiB.

In general, in 2020, if you are running your app in the cloud on small or medium instances, which don't have a lot of cores, I would recommend setting p to 1 or 2, that is, using only one or two threads for computation. Note that some implementations of scrypt do not implement multithreading, and instead run computations sequentially rather than in parallel in multiple threads.

How much memory should you use? Basically, use as much of it as you can afford, but not less than 16 MiB. Due to the design of scrypt, anything less than that can be optimized by attackers to compute hashes faster. I would recommend at least 64 MiB for cases when you can't afford larger resources, and more than that if you have some money to spend on better hardware. Also, make sure you don't overload your hardware by trying to compute more hashes than you can afford at the same time. For example, if you have 10 users signing up simultaneously, you will have to compute 10 hashes, which consumes around 2.5 GiB when using 256 MiB for each, so make sure to adjust the parameters according to what you can afford and queue password hash computation. Since scrypt depends on memory latency, you don't want to compute a lot of hashes at the same time, making each computation longer.

Scrypt has the same issue with long passwords as PBKDF2, because it uses one-round PBKDF2 internally before the memory-hard computation:

```
x = PBKDF2-HMAC-SHA-256(password, salt, iterations=1)
y = MemoryHardMagic(x)
hash = PBKDF2-HMAC-SHA-256(password, y, iterations=1)
```

If the password is longer than SHA-256 block size — 64 bytes — then there will be another password, SHA-256(password), that is equal to it. This is normally not a problem for most systems, but you should know about it in case it's not acceptable for your system. You can protect against it by prehashing, as described in Prehashing for scrypt and bcrypt.

Scrypt specification is available at https://www.tarsnap.com/scrypt.html

scrypt implementations

- Go: `golang.org/x/crypto/scrypt`

- JavaScript (browser): `@stablelib/scrypt` on npm

- JavaScript (Node.js): `scrypt` on npm

- Ruby: `OpenSSL::KDF.scrypt` from the `openssl` standard library module

- Python: `scrypt` from the `hashlib` standard library module

- Java: https://github.com/wg/scrypt

Some implementations of scrypt accept log_2N instead of N, so for our example with 256 MiB, you will pass not 262144, but log_2 262144, which is 18. Make sure to understand what your implementation accepts. Passing log_2N instead of N would make your hash very fast and easily attacked, while passing N to an implementations that expects log_2N will probably lead to freezes when it tries to allocate that much memory.

Some implementations, for instance, Sodium (https://download.libsodium.org/doc/advanced/scrypt), instead of N, r, p, take *opslimit* and *memlimit*: the actual N and p are derived from them, while r is fixed to 8.

yescrypt

Yescrypt is a modified version of scrypt created by Alexander Peslyak for the Password Hashing Competition. It didn't win, but received special recognition. It fixes some scrypt quirks and introduces additional features: ROM hardness, hash encryption, and output formatting. You can think of it as a better and easier to use version of scrypt.

ROM hardness is a feature that makes hash computation require a large amount of fixed memory, stored for example in RAM or SSD. For the dictionary attack, the attackers would need the same ROM, which increases the cost of building the specialized cracking hardware, and makes using botnets of low-memory devices for password cracking not as attractive. Since the attackers would need to steal the whole ROM, and downloading thousands of gigabytes usually takes more effort and time than leaking password hashes, security breaches can be detected early.

Hash encryption makes it easy for the hash computation to require a secret key for accessing the hash. Implementation of hash encryption is discussed in Peppering and encrypting hashes, but you don't need it, because yescrypt has it built in. It uses a custom block cipher built from the internals of scrypt/yescrypt, which accepts 32-byte keys.

Yescrypt can format the hash in a way similar to bcrypt, encoding the algorithm, the salt, and the hash into a single text string. Refer to Encoding and storing password hashes for details.

The reference implementation of yescrypt can also compute standard scrypt hashes.

The downside of yescrypt is that it doesn't have a lot of bindings to other programming languages yet.

Yescrypt is available from https://www.openwall.com/yescrypt/.

Argon2

Argon2 is a password hashing and key derivation function that won the Password Hashing Competition in 2015. It was created by Alex Biryukov, Daniel Dinu, and Dmitry Khovratovich. Argon2 is both memory- and computationally hard, and unlike scrypt can be separately configured for how much memory it consumes and how much time the computation takes. It is also better at defending against time-memory tradeoff attacks. Argon2 internally uses a variant of BLAKE2 cryptographic hash function, modified to use more circuits inside the CPU for computation.

Argon2 comes in three variants: Argon2i, Argon2d, and Argon2id.

Argon2i is stronger against side-channel attacks since it uses secret-independent memory accesses but it is weaker against time-memory tradeoff attacks.

Argon2d is not side-channel safe, however, it provides better defense against time-memory tradeoff attacks. It is mainly recommended for use in cryptocurrencies or when the attacker doesn't have access to the machine, while Argon2i is better suited for running in virtualized environments, where attackers can potentially get access to the timing information of the memory accesses.

Argon2id is a combination of both, somewhat side-channel resistant, but retaining most of the time-memory tradeoff attack defenses. For server-based user authentication, use Argon2id.

Argon2 is optimized for 64-bit Intel/AMD processors. It uses 64-bit integer arithmetic, 32-bit multiplications, and other tricks to make it consume as much processor resources as possible, so that you, the defender, is not too disadvantaged compared to the attacker that uses GPU or builds an ASIC-based device — the cost of such ASIC compared to the cost of just using the generic CPU would not give any advantage to the attacker, so the attacker will have to use the same Intel/AMD CPU as you do.

You should not use Argon2 implementation written in pure JavaScript or another scripting language — while the scrypt implementation is slower than the native one, the gap between the native Argon2 and the JavaScript Argon2 is much larger, since JavaScript doesn't have optimized 64-bit arithmetic or 32-bit integer multiplications. WebAssembly version, though, should work with acceptable performance. (See Client-side password prehashing for details on the client-side use of password hashing functions.)

Argon2 cost parameters are the memory cost in kilobytes, the number of iterations it should go over the memory, and the parallelism. While with scrypt you cannot adjust computational cost without it affecting the memory cost, Argon2 can do it, so it is more flexible. Argon2 can also accept a secret key and associated data. If you want to use the peppering technique discussed in the Peppering and encrypting hashes section, with Argon2 you do not have to invent your own construction, instead you can use the pepper as a secret key input. Associated data is not generally needed for our purpose: it can separate domains of different uses of the password.

Like bcrypt and yescrypt, Argon2 has an encoding specification that gives you a text string with all the encoded information needed to verify passwords without storing parameters separately. Here's the example of an Argon2 hash:

```
$argon2i$v=19$m=65536,t=2,p=4$c29tZXNhbHQ$RdescudvJCsgt3u
b+b+dWRWJTmaaJObG
```

See the Encoding and storing password hashes section.

Argon2 specification is available at https://github.com/P-H-C/phc-winner-argon2/blob/master/argon2-specs.pdf

Argon2 implementations

See https://github.com/p-h-c/phc-winner-argon2 for the reference C implementation and bindings to it for many programming languages.

Sodium includes Argon2id and Argon2i implementations: https://download.libsodium.org/doc/password_hashing.

Make sure to use an implementation of the Argon2 v1.3 specification.

Goodbye, rainbow tables

You may have heard about scary rainbow tables that hackers use to crack hashes. A rainbow table is a data structure that crackers built to optimize dictionary attacks on hashed passwords in the olden times when most web developers didn't know how to hash passwords (unlike Unix developers who knew this since the late 1970s[11]). Rainbow tables are nothing to worry about with password hashing functions because they include salt. That's it.[12]

Prehashing for scrypt and bcrypt

Prehashing is a trick to protect against bcrypt's and scrypt's long password issues. Instead of directly hashing passwords with a password hashing function, first, we prehash the password with a fast cryptographic hash function to turn it into a fixed-length short string and then use the result as a password input for the password hashing function.

Instead of using a cryptographic hash function as-is, we will use the HMAC construction[13], HMAC-SHA-256. "But you said there were problems caused by HMAC!" Yes, indeed, but we will use it in a way that avoids these problems.

First, I'd like to introduce you to domain separation. You see, most systems are complex, they are written by different teams, and it's hard to track down how one piece of data that's used in one part of the system is used in another part. Sometimes using a piece of data in a way that you thought was safe would actually be unsafe if the same data is used somewhere else. This is a common problem in cryptographic protocols. For example, if one part of a protocol uses a SHA-256 hash of a secret key to encrypt some data, but another part exposes the SHA-256 hash of it to verify something, the protocol is broken: you can just use the exposed hash to decrypt data, without even knowing the actual key! Domain separation can prevent this: basically, you attach meaning to data depending on which part of the system you use it in, similar to types in a programming language. In other terms, with domain separation, you clone a single cryptographic function into many independent functions.

Here's a simple domain separation example:

```
> hash1 = HMAC-SHA-256(key="Mocha Joe", data="scones")
790920dfad8341838efbf0e8635056a41da93c13d9080dd302...

> hash2 = HMAC-SHA-256(key="Latte Larry", data="scones")
914810708d1613a5652bf67985da46ce1d6522a4396a601b33...
```

We used literal strings "Mocha Joe" and "Latte Larry" as keys for HMAC and the same data input, "scones", for both. Since the keys are different, hash1 will always differ from hash2 even for the same input data. Keys serve as domain separation constants.

Why do we need this for prehashing? If we just used SHA-256(password), it would be fine... until we decide to use SHA-256(password) somewhere else in the system for a different task, and then we'd have to audit every usage of it. Or someone might have used the same password for a service that hashed passwords with SHA-256 and those hashes were leaked. Without domain separation, the attacker can just use the hash to log in to our system without even cracking the password. So, for prehashing we'll use domain separation with a clear description of our system and our task:

```
prehash = HMAC-SHA-256(key="Prehashing for example.com",
data=password)
```

In our case, the HMAC key is a literal string describing the operation and the place where we use it.[14] If we don't use the same domain separation string in other places, we'll have a unique prehash for the password.

Now, as we mentioned in the bcrypt section, to prevent implementation shenanigans related to C NUL-terminated strings, we encode the prehash into ASCII characters using hex encoding:

```
prehash = HexEncode(HMAC-SHA-256(key="Prehashing for
example.com", data=password))
```

There you have it, a 64-character string that you can use as the password for bcrypt or scrypt.

If you intend to use the "peppering" of password hashes (described in Peppering and encrypting hashes), you can feed two birds with one scone by using the pepper in place of the domain separation string. Since the pepper is your own secret, the hashes will be unique to your system.

A word of warning. You probably don't need prehashing! For bcrypt, you can just limit the password length to 72 bytes. For scrypt, having a possibility of accessing your app with two passwords if one of them is longer than 64 bytes is something you're unlikely to have to care about; the only concern with it is if someone had a 65+ byte password and reused it on another website where it was hashed with unsalted SHA-256... I suspect it is rare. Adding more code that deals with cryptography, which is difficult to implement correctly, is a huge responsibility and there is always a risk of introducing a horrible bug that will break your authentication. You've been warned! Don't play with fire.

Peppering and encrypting hashes

Peppering is an additional protection for password hashes that makes them impossible to crack without knowing the secret key. It works by adding a secret input, called "pepper", to the hashing function.

A pepper is actually a secret key, just with a funky name. It should be a strong cryptographic key: 32 randomly generated bytes is ideal. The pepper is kept in the memory of the server that does authentication. It provides protection for the cases when the attacker can access the password hashes database, but doesn't have access to the application server (for example, when a database backup leaks or the database is compromised with SQL injection). It is also useful when your database is in the cloud and the database provider suffers a breach.

Of the mentioned password hashing functions only Argon2 has a built-in way to add pepper. However, it can be added to any function in one of the following ways:

1. Pre-hashing with the pepper before[15] password hashing.

2. Concatenating the pepper with the salt.

Pre-hashing with pepper can be done using HMAC, for example, HMAC-SHA-256, where the pepper is the secret key. The result is then used as a password input to the hashing function, for example:

```
prehash = HMAC-SHA-256(pepper, password)
hash = scrypt(prehash, salt, N, r, p)
```

Note that as warned above, for bcrypt and implementations of other password hashes that accept NUL-terminated strings, you will need to encode the prehash before inputting it into the password hash (for example, encode it in hex or Base64).

Prehashing suits bcrypt more, since it also solves the limited password length problem, and since the length of salt in bcrypt is fixed, so concatenation will not work with it.

For PBKDF2, scrypt and yescrypt you can simply concatenate the pepper with the salt:

```
newSalt = CONCAT(pepper, salt)
hash = scrypt(prehash, newSalt, N, r, p)
```

In other words, if you have a 32-byte pepper and a 16-byte salt, you concatenate them into a single 48-byte array and use the result as the salt input for the password hashing function.

Don't forget that you should not store newSalt or the pepper along with the password — just store the original salt (before concatenation with the pepper).

For Argon2, just pass the pepper into the secret key input.

The pepper is not per-user, but a global value for all users. There's no point in overcomplicating this.

It is important to remember, that while peppering provides some additional protection, unless you use Argon2 as your password hash, it introduces more lines of code, which can lead to vulnerabilities, so if you are unsure about it, skip it. Also, if the pepper value is lost, all hashes become useless, so you will not be able to authenticate users and will have to reset their passwords. Carefully consider if this additional protection is worth the complexity.

Peppering is one-way: even if you know the pepper and the hash, you cannot get the "unpeppered" hash back. This complicates hash database maintenance: rotating the pepper without users re-logging in is impossible, updating the hash cost offline is more complicated, merging two databases of hashes with different peppers requires storing a pepper identifier for each hash.

A different way to introduce a secret key into the scheme is to encrypt the hash. This way, if you know the key and the encrypted hash, you can decrypt it to get the original hash back. For our purposes, it provides basically the same protection, but more options for the future.

Hash encryption works like this:

```
hash = scrypt(password, salt, N, r, p)
encryptedHash = ENCRYPT(secretKey, hash)
```

First, you calculate the password hash normally. Then you encrypt the hash and store the result of encryption. To verify the password, decrypt the encrypted hash with the same secret key to get the original hash, and then compare the hashes as you would normally do.

What should you use for encryption? For simplicity, choose an authenticated encryption with a random nonce: AES-GCM, as implemented in standard libraries of many programming languages, or ChaCha20-Poly1305 or XSalsa20-Poly1305 (for example, from Sodium). You will need to generate a random nonce and append it to the encrypted hash, which will also contain the authentication tag, thus your password hashes will grow in size — by 28 bytes for AES-GCM and ChaCha20-Poly1305 or by 40 bytes for XSalsa20-Poly1305.

Encryption is easier to get wrong than HMAC, so approach it carefully. Yescrypt comes with its own built-in cipher, so you don't need an external encryption function for it, just provide the secret key.

Since peppering and encrypting hashes are used for the same purpose of making the hashes in the database depend on a secret key, don't do both: choose either peppering or encrypting. If your password hashing function is bcrypt, use peppering, since it also fixes the password length issue. If you use Argon2, use peppering, since it's built-in. If you use yescrypt, use encryption, since it's built-in.

Remember that it is easy to introduce vulnerabilities when writing encryption code. Carefully consider the risk of doing something wrong versus a slight advantage against the attackers.

Hash length

PBKDF2, scrypt, and Argon2 allow you to request a practically unlimited number of output bytes, so how long should your hashes be? The hash should be long enough to not cause a collision with another hash (which will simplify dictionary attacks and allow one user to authenticate with a different user's password). It shouldn't be too long since there is no more security to be gained after some length.

16 to 32 bytes is enough. More than that is useless (and for PBKDF2 even dangerous). I usually recommend 32 bytes, because while 16 bytes is plenty, some programmers mistake this requirement to

mean 16 bytes of hex-encoded output (which would result in an unsafe 8-byte hash). When it's 32 bytes, even if they use 32 hex chars, it would be twice shorter, but still safe.

With bcrypt, you don't control the hash output length, so stick with whatever output it gives you (which also includes identifier, version, salt, and the 23-byte hash, as discussed in the next section.

Encoding and storing password hashes

All password hashing functions described in this book, except for bcrypt, by default output only hash bytes. This is because they are also key derivation functions — functions that turn a password into a key suitable for ciphers (e.g. a 128-bit key for AES or a 256-bit key for ChaCha). This output is a pseudorandom uniformly distributed sequence of bytes. However, for web services authentication, you also want to store salt and cost parameters. The easiest way to do it is to create separate columns in the database for these values.

For example, for scrypt, you will have the following table:

- N — integer — memory cost

- r — integer — internal block size

- p — integer — parallelism

- salt — 32-character hex string

- hash — 32-character hex string

(Notice that salt is 16 randomly generated bytes encoded as a 32-

character hex string, and *hash* is a 16-byte output of scrypt encoded as 32 hex characters.)

If you store it this way, you will find it easier to upgrade hashes. For example, if you initially had parallelism $p = 1$, and after a year of success, you purchased a new multi-core server specifically for running password hashes, you may want to increase the parallelism to 4. You can simply query your database for $p <= 4$ to estimate how many users will need to be upgraded.

The alternative way, the way bcrypt and your Unix-based personal computer stores hashes, is to encode the information about the salt, the cost, and the hash into a string, from which it can be extracted. Usually, the format also encodes the function type and its version. For example, the output of bcrypt may look like this:

```
$2b$10$Mr6lCXuw0frE71i7MRNJR.qc4qjbmf6kIGMITklJ.ZVUiQVFuE
X3y
```

It stores the bcrypt identifier (2b), the cost (10) and the salt randomness (Mr6lCXuw0frE71i7MRNJR.). The final part is the actual hash. This format is easy to handle: you don't need to change your database schema if you decide to use a different hashing function, just use "password_hash" column, which will include everything the password hashing function needs to calculate and compare the hash. The disadvantage is that you cannot easily query the cost, or check if you accidentally reused the same salt — you will need to go through each row in the password database to decode this information.

Argon2 and yescrypt come with functions that can produce such strings.

There's no universally accepted format for PBKDF2 and scrypt, although there were efforts to create such a standard (which, of course, resulted in many incompatible formats). If you use scrypt, you can switch to yescrypt, or at least borrow the encoding function from it.

Hash upgrades

With growing computing power and memory, you want to periodically upgrade hashes of your users with increased cost parameters to consume more CPU or RAM. In 2000, the cost of 8 was considered good enough for bcrypt, but now the hash can be computed a lot faster. Something that previously took half a second now may take only less than a hundred milliseconds to compute. You may also want to switch to a different hashing algorithm.

If you followed the previous sections on password hashing, then you ran benchmarks and adjusted the cost accordingly. Schedule periodic re-testing of parameters at least once every two-three years, or when you purchase a new generation of hardware. When you discover that your hashing cost no longer fits the target, you need to upgrade hashes.

Once you decide to upgrade hashes, the first thing to do is to increase the cost when creating new accounts or changing passwords. Then implement the following system: the next time a user logs in, after checking the password with the current hash, re-hash the password with new parameters and replace the current hash with the upgraded one.

The downside of upgrading the hash only when the user logs in is that until this happens, the hash will remain stored with the old cost. If this continues for a long time, consider upgrading it in-place using the current hash as input.

Rehashing passwords without user intervention is complicated, so I don't recommend doing this unless the current cost is too low or the hash function is insecure. It works like this:

1. Take the current hash and use is as a password input for the hash with the new cost and a new salt.

2. Store the old and the new parameters and salts, and the new hash, and flag this account to indicate that its hash has been upgraded.

3. Remove the old hash.

To verify the password, if the flag indicating that this is an upgraded hash is set, hash the password with the previous salt and parameters, then hash the result again with the new salt and para-meters. Compare the result with the stored new hash. If you don't want to hash twice every time the user logs in, you may now want to switch to the new hash directly as described above, if the pass-word is correct.

The same method can be used to switch to a different hashing algorithm.

Client-side password prehashing

Normally, your server receives passwords submitted by the user as-is. You will hash them as soon as they arrive and then deal with hashes. However, passwords may stay in memory for some time until they are freed and overwritten by other data. They may unintentionally end up in logs, or written to disk, or sent to some third-party telemetry service.

Since most web apps are no longer simple HTML pages and require JavaScript to work, wouldn't it be nice to have some preprocessing of passwords on the client-side? Then we could send them to the server in the hashed form. Will it improve security? Also, could we offload at least some of hashing cost to the client?

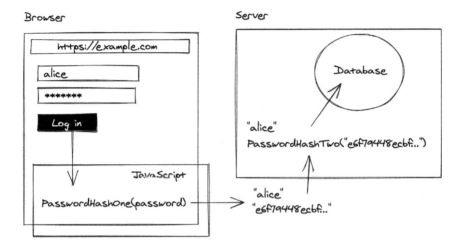

As always, there are two sides of the coin. Sure, this may improve security, but it will also introduce a lot of complexity, and you might unintentionally create a vulnerability somewhere. For most cases, I would recommend against any client-side processing. If you still want it, here is how to do it securely.

First of all, remember that whatever you do with the password on the client side, the result will become the actual password from the server's point of view. If you hash the password, from the server's point of view the hash of the password *is* the password. If the attacker gets the original password before hashing, they can log in to the server. If the attacker gets the hashed password, they also can log in to the server by skipping your client-side processing. Thus, on the server, the prehashed password should still be hashed again, with the password hashing function (however, depending on the parameters you choose, you can relax some computation or memory requirements).

Secondly, salting on the client side is tricky. Remember that when the server stores a hashed password, it also stores a salt for the password hashing function. This salt is known only to the server, and attackers cannot run any precomputation without knowing it. If you do the client-side prehashing, there is no salt. You cannot simply generate it and store it in the cookie or local storage — the user won't be able to log in on another device without knowing it. Even if you create some kind of a protocol when the user has to store or remember the salt, the whole password authentication scheme doesn't make sense at all — call this salt a secret key, and use the appropriate protocol for authentication.

There are two ways to deal with salts on the client side. The first way is to take the username as the salt. Since the user needs to remember and enter their username anyway, you can use it as a salt for the client-side hashing. However, this has security weaknesses: this salt will be known to the attacker (thus the attacker will be able to precompute the hash), it is low-entropy, and it can't be changed when the user changes their password, so all the user's passwords will be hashed with the same salt (which means that the hash will be the same if the passwords are the same for that user). Still, you are going to use the proper salt on the server anyway, so the server's password database is secure. I like this solution for its simplicity.

The second way to deal with the client-side salt is to let the server store it and then, before logging in, request it from the server by username and use it for hashing. This is a more complicated solution, but it ensures that when the password is changed, the salt changes and the hash becomes different even for the same password. However, it still retains the attacker's advantage: since the user cannot be authenticated before they request the salt from the server, an attacker can also request salts for the users they want to target and precompute hashes.

Here's the algorithm:

1. When the user enters their username and the password, the app requests the user's salt from the server corresponding.

2. The server looks up the salts database for the username and responds with the stored salt. (Note that this a client-side salt, which is different from the password hash database salt.)

3. The client then computes a password hash from the user's password and the received salt, and then sends the result as a password, along with the username to log in.

This approach is more complex, so I only recommend using it for the cases when you need to derive client-side keys for end-to-end encryption. For a simple client-side prehashing, you can use username as the salt.

It is important to stress that you cannot authenticate the salt or the cost parameters that the client receives from the server. I once discovered such vulnerability in the security audit for a note-taking app. The app developers stored the salt correctly, however, the security experts recommended to protect the salt with an authentication tag created with the password. In that case, the attacker who requests the salt also gets a kind of the password hash they can verify their guesses against — the authentication tag. (After I pointed out the vulnerability, the security experts withdrew this recommendation, of course.)

There is actually a better way to deal with salts — see the OPAQUE protocol[16]. However, it is quite complicated, and there are no easy-to-use implementations of it yet, and you don't really need it for the simple authentication with passwords, so it won't be discussed.

What about cost parameters? You can also either fix them for the lifetime of your app or store them on the server and then request them as described above with the salt. If you do so, make sure to check that the cost parameters you received from the server are reasonable — not too low, and not too high (otherwise, if the server goes crazy or gets attacked, it will be able to cause the denial of service for the client, making the app or the browser tab freeze or waste a lot of memory.)

What hash function should you use for the client-side prehashing? One of the password hashes I described in the book, of course! You can even use different password hashing functions on the client and on the server if you like. Modern browsers that implement the WebCrypto standard come with PBKDF2[17]. There are also JavaScript implementations of bcrypt and scrypt (in fact, I wrote one specifically for the client-side prehashing to be compatible with even older browsers — see https://github.com/dchest/scrypt-async-js). I do not recommend using Argon2 for this purpose, since its implementation in JavaScript is a lot slower than a fast native implementation, giving a huge advantage to the attacker. (WebAssembly implementation should be fine.)

When you're done with hashing, the result of the hashing function becomes the password. For PBKDF2 and scrypt, derive 32 bytes and encode those bytes into the plaintext format, such as hex or Base64, and send the result to the server as you would normally do with the password.

On the server, calculate the password hash with the hash you received from the client as a password, and a separate server-only salt.

Resetting passwords

People often forget passwords, so your app needs a way to restore access to their accounts. This means that people need to access their accounts without a password. Hm... this doesn't sound like a bright idea! It isn't, indeed. In a perfectly secure world, people would have to forget about ever getting back inside if they lose their password. Your support staff's conversation with them would be easy: "Sorry, we can't do anything. We'll continue charging your card, though! Thanks, bye!"

In apps that don't use end-to-end encryption, username and password are used to verify the identity of the user — to ensure that the user that's logging in is, in fact, the same user that signed up. If there is another way for us to verify this, we can use it as an alternative way to let them access the account and reset their forgotten password. The most common way is to use email. Users ask to reset their password, we send them a link, we pretend we delivered the email securely and that it is them, the original user, and not someone who hacked into their email, not the postmaster of the email service they use, certainly not NSA or FSB, is now trying to reset their password, and we let them click on that link and create a new password. That's how it works for most apps, and we can't really do better with the tools we currently have. We need these users, or, rather, we need their money!

The olden days were even worse: services stored passwords in plaintext and just sent them by email when requested. It is bad because, apart from the fact they stored passwords unhashed, you'd never know if someone else, who intercepted this email, also accessed your account.

Anyway, how to implement password resets?

Your service presents a form where the user can enter their email address. If you want to keep the email undisclosed (see Usernames vs email addresses), don't immediately report whether the email address was found or not — just say that if this email belongs to the account, the address will receive a message with instructions on how to reset the password. If the user with this email address doesn't exist in the system, simply don't send anything to anyone. If it does, send the password reset instructions that include the link.

To create a reset link, first, mark the account as being in the state of password reset, and generate a random token, similar to the one discussed in Sessions and Universal confirmation system: a 16-byte identifier and a 16-byte verifier stored in the hashed form; combine the token into a single string and put it into the link. Make sure this token has a short expiration period (half an hour would be plenty — if the user fails to create a new password during that time, they can always request the reset again).

For better usability, you can allow a single user to have many outstanding password resets. If they request the password reset twice without acting on any of them, they should be able to click the link in any of the messages (at least, until they expire). However, when the user sets a new password or when they successfully log in with the old password before they clicked the link, make sure to delete all of their reset tokens. After they set a new password, delete all of the sessions except for the current one, and possibly, all verifications.

Here's the detailed algorithm:

1. When the user submits the username or the email address for the password reset, find if this user exists. If you're hiding the existence of email addresses, immediately display a message that says that the email will be sent to this address if it exists in the system, and schedule the rest of the steps as a separate action to prevent timing attacks (otherwise, it may be easy to tell if you've found the user or not by measuring how long it takes for the server to respond, since the server won't perform

the rest of the steps for the negative result).

2. When the user is found, generate a 16-byte identifier and a 16-byte verifier, hash the verifier with SHA-256 and store the hash, the expiration time, the user identifier (as a secondary index, so that later you can find all tokens for the user), and whatever other information you need, in the database indexed by the identifier.

3. Combine the identifier and the original verifier into a single string (token), put it into the corresponding URL and send it by email. Make sure to never reveal this token anywhere else! The email message may look like this:

```
Hello,

We received a request to reset your [App Name]
password. If you didn't request it, please ignore this
message.

To reset your password, click this link:

https://example.com/reset?token=XXXXXX…

The link will be valid until MM, DD hh:mm.
```

If the user doesn't reset the password and instead logs in with their current password, remove all password reset entries for them from the password resets database.

When the user clicks on this link, do the following on the server:

1. Split the token into the identifier and the verifier.

2. Look up the password reset record using the identifier. If it's not found, report an error (something like "token not found or expired") and stop.

3. Hash the verifier and compare the result with the hash stored in the record. If they don't match, report an error.

4. Check the expiration time. If it's past the current time, report an error and stop.

5. Finally, display the form to set up a new password for the user. This form will submit to a different endpoint (or to the same endpoint, using the POST method), so include the original token as a hidden input to it.

When the user submits a new password via the form, follow the same steps to find and verify this token, but now instead of displaying the form, actually set the new password for the user. After that, remove all password reset records for this user and invalidate all their sessions (see the Sessions chapter). Respond by logging in the user — that is, by creating a new session. In fact, you can combine the code that invalidates all this stuff into a single function that is triggered when the password is set — we'll also need to do it when the user changes their password while in the logged in state.

Alternatively, instead of using a different database table for password resets, you can put the verifier hash into the users table, and instead of a separate identifier for the record, use the user identifier for lookup.

Changing passwords

To change the password, the user must be logged in. To prevent an attacker who gains temporary access to their device from changing their password, they must also enter their current password.

When the user submits the password change request, the server must verify the current password just like it does when logging in the user by hashing it and comparing the hashes, and then hash and save the new password. Before that, you may want to compare the new password with the old one (before hashing) in order to avoid performing the useless operation, although you'd probably want to do it client-side.

If the password change form has a hidden username input (to improve compatibility with password managers), make sure to *ignore* the submitted username on the server — only use the user identifier from the current session.

All sessions and password reset requests must be invalidated when the password is changed.

Some services keep a few hashes of previous passwords and verify the new password with them. This is to prevent the user from entering the same password when changing it. Such services will display an error saying that the user cannot use the previous password. I would advise against this practice. First of all, this practice was used to enforce password rotation — see the Against enforced password rotation section for discussion on why it is bad. Secondly, in case of the hash database leak, the attackers get the previous password hashes. Usually users change passwords if they discover that the ones they had were not secure, which means that those passwords were likely to have a low entropy, and would be easier for the attackers to crack. Sure, they will not be able to log in to your service with the old password, but who knows where else it was used. Just keep the hash of the current password, don't create artificial limits when they are unnecessary.

Against enforced password rotation

Enforced periodical password rotation was once popular, and, unfortunately, is still practiced. Every month or so users are asked to change their passwords. This is a bad practice that should be stopped.

The original thinking was that password rotation is useful for minimizing the time between attackers learning the current password and the time they will no longer be able to log in with it. If the password database is leaked, it will become useless in a month, when the users change their passwords.

It was discovered, though, that in the real world it doesn't work and only annoys people by making them change their passwords: research showed that instead of creating a completely new password, users just stuffed a digit or changed a few letters in the current one. The passwords are never really rotated, they are just permuted.

Password rotation was promoted by NIST (United States National Institute of Standards and Technology), which develops and publishes many security and cryptography standards that have a lot of influence. However, NIST no longer recommends this practice and even the person who originally introduced it to the standard now regrets it[18].

Only enforce password rotation when you discover a leak. Be aware, though, that users won't create completely different passwords for their accounts. Such is life.

Secret questions

Secret questions are controversial in the security community. They gained their bad reputation mostly because in the early 2000s major web apps used them as the only way to reset passwords. The questions were often simple: a person's birthday or mother maiden name, so it was not hard to find this information about most people, and reset their passwords.

Secret questions won't help with targeted attacks but can be useful as an additional measure to slow down attackers in some instances, for example, by adding them as a required step to password resets by email. Again, an *additional* measure, not the only one! You still have to use email for verification.

Do not ask questions the answers to which are easily found. Ask questions that are truly personal: the ones that are unlikely to be published by the user on the web. Questions, of course, should be inclusive and not offensive.

Answers to the questions are low-entropy secret data. What other secret data is usually low-entropy? Passwords. So, protect answers in the same way as passwords: do not store them as plaintext, instead, hash them with a password hashing function, with a random salt. Usually, answers contain even less entropy than passwords, so they can be more easily cracked with the dictionary attack — choose a higher cost of computation for the hash function.

It's not easy for users to remember how they typed their answers when they suddenly need to re-type them a few years later, so you need to normalize them. Remove extra spaces (leading, trailing, and more than one space between words) and fold case (to upper or lower). Hash the normalized answers with the password hashing function and store the results. To verify, normalize the answer entered by the user, hash it, and then compare the hash with the stored one.

In the password reset flow, ask secret questions *after* the user clicks on the reset link in the email message, not before, to prevent anyone else from guessing the answers.

—

[5] NIST Special Publication 800-63B: Digital Identity Guidelines, 5.1.1.2 Memorized Secret Verifiers, https://pages.nist.gov/800-63-3/sp800-63b.html#-5112 -memorized-secret-verifiers

[6] Unicode FAQ: Normalization, http://www.unicode.org/faq/normalization.html

[7] The proper name for it would actually be PBKDF2-HMAC-SHA-2-256. Now, if you'd like some fun, we also have truncated SHA-2 variants, and if you were to use them (don't), you'd have PBKDF2-HMAC-SHA-2-512/256. Nice? Just don't say it aloud, it's an ancient cryptographic spell.

[8] SHA-1 is probably still the most popular hash function, but we won't consider it because it is broken. Do not use it anywhere. If you happen to use it, migrate from it as soon as possible. If you want to argue that it is still safe for a specific purpose, you're are contributing to the sorry state of security in this world, and I hate you.

[9] Credit to @CodesInChaos: https://twitter.com/CodesInChaos/status/422073818228613121

[10] Block size is a size of the internal state of the hash function. It's different from the output size: for SHA-256 the output size is 32 bytes, the block size is 64 bytes, for SHA-512 it's 64 and 128 bytes respectively.

[11] See the 1979 paper by Robert Morris and Ken Thompson, Password Security: A Case History. I've collected some early password hashing functions here: https://github.com/dchest/historic-password-hashes

[12] If you want to learn how rainbow tables work, Wikipedia has a great article: https://en.wikipedia.org/wiki/Rainbow_table

[13] If you use BLAKE2 or BLAKE3 hash functions, you don't need HMAC for domain separation: BLAKE2 includes a personalization parameter that you can use as the domain separation value, BLAKE3 has a key derivation mode that includes a context string.

[14] While you can use strings of any length, I don't recommend making them longer than the hash block size (64 bytes for HMAC-SHA-256) to avoid unnecessary double-hashing: see the PBKDF2 section for details.

[15] Why not add the pepper *after* hashing the password? The attacker can precompute guesses before they learn the pepper. When the pepper leaks, they

can use it to quickly check the guesses. If you use the pepper before the expensive password hashing (or along with the salt), the attacker can't even start cracking passwords without it.

[16] See OPAQUE: An Asymmetric PAKE Protocol Secure Against Pre-Computation Attacks paper (https://eprint.iacr.org/2018/163) and Matthew Green's blog post: https://blog.cryptographyengineering.com/2018/10/19/lets-talk-about-pake/

[17] SubtleCrypto.deriveBits, https://developer.mozilla.org/en-US/docs/Web/API/SubtleCrypto/deriveBits

[18] The Wall Street Journal: The Man Who Wrote Those Password Rules Has a New Tip: N3v$r M1^d!, https://www.wsj.com/articles/the-man-who-wrote-those-password-rules-has-a-new-tip-n3v-r-m1-d-1502124118

Multi-factor authentication

What is multi-factor authentication?

Multi-factor authentication is an additional measure to protect accounts in case of a user's password leak via phishing, malware, or due to password reuse. It requires a secondary secure channel or device to authenticate the user, such as a smartphone authenticator app or a hardware security key.

Authenticator apps generate one-time codes, or OTP ("one-time password", even though they are not really passwords). The user enters their code after authenticating with the password to log in to their account. Since the codes are typed by users, just like passwords, they are vulnerable to phishing: an attacker-controlled web site presents a fake log in form, with which it gathers user's information required for logging in, including the one-time code, and immediately uses this information with the real web app to get into the user's account.

The most used standard for one-time code authentication is TOTP — Time-based One-Time Password. It is supported by Google Authenticator, Authy, and most other authenticator apps.

Security keys use USB, NFC or Bluetooth to communicate with browsers, which perform secure authentication using public-key cryptography. Security keys make phishing attacks impossible, since signatures created for one origin URL will not verify on another. The security keys are also safe against keyloggers that steal one-time codes but are helpless against malware that steals sessions after logging in, or the malware specifically designed to request signatures from security keys.

Multi-factor authentication is not only an additional security measure, but it is also an additional burden for users: they have to keep two devices available for signing in, retype codes, and deal with consequences of losing devices. To improve usability, it is important to let users remember devices on which they performed authentication for some time and not ask them for the second factor every time they log in on these devices.

Two-step or two-factor?

There are two terms to describe the process of requiring something other than password to log in: *two-factor authentication* (2FA, or *multi-factor*, MFA) and *two-step verification* (2SV). Technically, they describe different things. Two-factor authentication requires the presence of an actual second *factor* — usually a device, such as a security key, while two-step verification can use email, SMS, etc. The difference is subtle: with two-factor there should be a second thing without which it is impossible to log in. SMS is not a second thing because an attacker can intercept it.

Most people don't care about subtle differences when talking about either two-factor authentication or two-step verification: whatever it is, the second factor is considered something that is not a password. While it's nice to have precise terminology, it only confuses users.

Rate limiting

Rate limiting is very important for two-factor authentication with codes: without rate limiting, it's utterly broken. Since the TOTP or recovery codes are short, if you do not limit the rate of guessing, it will be possible for the attacker to bruteforce the code.

Since two-factor authentication happens after the user (or the attacker) correctly entered their password, your server knows what account to apply the rate limiting to, thus you should record the attempts for each user, and reset the count on successful authentication. Since rate limits are applied to the user account, not to the IP, this makes parallel guesses infeasible.

A good rate limit for two-factor authentication is exponential and, for better usability, applied after a few no-limit attempts. For example, after the first two attempts with no rate limiting, the next one can be tried after 1 second, then after 10 seconds, and so on.

Rate limiting of recovery code guesses is even more crucial. Unlike TOTP, recovery codes don't depend on time — they never change until the user decides to change them. You should limit the total number of unsuccessful attempts after which the account is locked since the attacker can slowly try many attempts until they succeed. Note that the lockdown can only be triggered by the attacker who already knows the user's password — it's not possible to lock users out of their accounts without knowing the password, so locking down accounts and requiring the user to change their password is a sensible thing to do.

TOTP

Time-based one-time token two-factor authentication is simple, just like quantum entanglement![19] Your server gives a secret key for the user's device to remember: they both share the same secret key (entangled). Then, when the user and the server are far apart, and the user needs a one-time code, their device computes an HMAC with this secret key from the current time and gives some part of it as digits (measurement). The server will do the same, and magically... *sorry*, scientifically, they both will come up with the same code!

Seriously though, since both have the same secret key, and they observe roughly the same time (rounded to a minute), and HMAC is a glorified hash, the hash of the same data (key and time) will be the same. That's how the server ensures that the code that the user entered is correct.

Unfortunately, people who standardized TOTP made a few mistakes[20] and unnecessary complications. First of all, they didn't just cut the hash and used the first or last bytes of it for codes — instead, they built a complicated extraction of bits from the hash, even though it is not necessary for a secure cryptographic hash function since it outputs a uniform sequence of bits. Secondly, they decided to use the SHA-1 hash function, which was already considered broken[21] at the time TOTP was standardized. Finally, their method of turning the hash output into the sequence of digits has modulo bias (see the Randomness section), making the already small output contain even fewer useful bits. Sigh!

Anyway, there are many libraries that take care of generating TOTP codes that you can use to avoid implementing it from scratch. You can read RFC 6238[22] if you want to do it, but we'll focus on the protocol, not the cryptographic primitives.

Here's how to implement 2FA with TOTP:

1. Generate a secret key on the server and store it in the database record for the user's account.

2. Output the secret key as QR code and also allow to display it as-is so that the user can either scan or manually input it into their authenticator app.

3. Ask the user to enter a code from the app and verify that the code is correct.

4. If the codes are correct, activate 2FA.

Allow the user to add more than one device for generating codes, and let them assign names to these devices. The devices must have different keys, so that if one was lost and the user deactivated it, the attackers who extracted the key from the lost device wouldn't be able to generate codes and get access to the user's account.

2FA codes must be verified only after the password verification succeeds. Usually, the code is entered in a separate form that is displayed after the log in form. (If you have a TOTP input in the same form as the password input, which I don't recommend, don't try to verify the code when the password is incorrect.) When verifying the OTP, don't strictly limit it to the exact minute, allow some slack for the timing differences. Even though most of devices and servers keep time synchronized with NTP, there still may be clock variations. Additionally, there is network latency to account for. On the server, if the current code is not valid, verify it against the code generated for the previous minute, and the future minute. Different apps may require different strictness.

Since the codes are low-entropy, they can be quite quickly guessed, so you will need to limit attempts to prevent guessing. Track the number of unsuccessful attempts: if it goes over the threshold, lock the account. (See the Rate limiting section for details.) Notify the user by email and don't allow any log in attempts for this account until the password is reset (remember that the attacker that can enter 2FA codes already knows the password).

SMS

SMS (text message system for mobile phones) is a popular method of two-step verification. When the user logs in, they are required to enter a short code that the service sends to their phone.

While it's better than nothing, SMS authentication is not as secure as other methods: there are real-world cases when attackers social-engineered telecom companies, ported the target's phone number to their SIM card and then received their messages. Apart from social engineering, SMS systems have other vulnerabilities.

SMS is also infinitely more expensive than TOTP or security keys: those are free, but you will have to pay for texts. So, only implement SMS authentication if you have no other choice for some reason.

If you already have the TOTP implementation and want to add SMS (why?), you can save on development efforts by reusing the TOTP system, except that instead of the user's device generating codes, your server would generate and send them to the user's phone by SMS.

Security keys: U2F, WebAuthn

Security keys that implement WebAuthn or U2F (Universal Second Factor) communicate with the user's web browser (or other client software), provide public keys specific for origins and sign challenges. Implementing two-factor authentication with WebAuthn/U2F in the browser requires client-side JavaScript code, which is quite simple and is only used to relay data between the security key and the server.

If you've heard about U2F, forget it — it's already dead. The new standard, WebAuthn, is being adopted by the industry. It's backward compatible with U2F keys — for instance, older U2F-only YubiKeys will work with WebAuthn — but U2F is not forward-compatible with WebAuthn, so newer WebAuthn-only keys will not work with U2F. New implementations should use WebAuthn to catch both types of keys.

WebAuthn is also becoming available on smartphones and computers equipped with with security chips, so there is no need for external keys. In this case, fingerprint or face recognition can be used to confirm authentication.

If you already use TOTP or plan to implement it in the future, do not force users to choose a single multi-factor authentication method: allow them to enable both if they want.

It's best to use existing libraries to implement WebAuthn rather than implementing it from scratch since it is quite complicated: you'll be dealing with low-level cryptographic primitives and tons of encodings (JSON, CBOR, COSE, DER, UTF-8, Base64, CPCN-SOASF[23]). My rule of thumb is: if you see "certificate" or "attestation" mentioned anywhere in the specification, you don't want to implement it from scratch; WebAuth specification has the "Packed attestation statement certificate requirements" section.

Here's a list of libraries you can use:

- Go: https://github.com/duo-labs/webauthn

- Java: https://github.com/Yubico/java-webauthn-server

- Python: https://github.com/duo-labs/py_webauthn

- Ruby: https://github.com/cedarcode/webauthn-ruby

A fresh list with more options is published at https://webauthn.io.

Read the documentation for a specific library to learn how to use it.

Since using security keys requires client-side code and interactive UI, it's best to implement the whole UI client-side and communicate with your server using an API.

Here's an overview of how it will work.

Registration

First, your users will need to register their security keys with your server. You should provide the ability to register more than one key to enable users to have backup keys. In fact, registering two keys is the recommended practice for users, since it minimizes the consequences of losing one of them. This is why most people don't use security keys.

Before you present a form to modify or add security keys, ask for the password. This is needed so that an attacker that gains temporary access to an active session won't be able to add a new security key or delete existing ones.

Present a form asking the user to insert their security key (or, for Bluetooth or NFC keys, have them ready). When the user confirms that they have the key ready to use, your client-side code calls your server's *initiate registration* API end-point to ask for a challenge.

The server receives the request and creates a challenge based on the user identifier for the current session. This challenge is then remembered and sent to the client.

Once the client receives the challenge, it asks the security key to create credentials with the challenge and then forwards the response to the server's *finish registration* end-point.

The server receives the security key's response from the client, verifies the response with the remembered challenge and adds the device, saving the received identifier and the public key.

At this point the user may be asked to assign a name to this key, which the server will store.

Authentication

After the user enters the correct password (the server must always verify the password before asking for the security key), the client asks the server to send the list of the registered security keys using the *initiate authentication* API end-point.

The server looks up the list of security keys for the user and generates and remembers a challenge. It sends the list of identifiers and the challenge to the client.

The client receives the list of security key identifiers and the challenge and calls the browser API with them. If the key from the identifiers list is present, the browser asks the user for the action (to press a button on the security key or to identify using the fingerprint or face recognition). The security key signs the challenge. The client then sends the result to the server's *finish authentication* end-point.

The server receives the security key response and verifies it. If verification is successful, the user is considered authenticated.

Resources

- WebAuthn Specification: https://www.w3.org/TR/webauthn/

- WebAuthn Guide: https://webauthn.guide/#authentication

- List of libraries that implement WebAuthn: https://webauthn.io

Recovery codes

Two-factor authentication is great for security, however, users may lose their 2FA devices, so they need a way to restore access to their account. A common way to do so is to generate recovery codes that users will write down on a piece of paper before they are allowed to enable multi-factor authentication. These codes can be used in place of a TOTP code or a security key to access the account and disable 2FA or add another device.

The requirements for recovery codes are:

1. An attacker must not be able to guess the code with a limited number of attempts.

2. They should be short enough to write down.

3. They must be single-use: once the code is used, it can't be used again.

4. Due to the 3rd requirement, a user should be given a few of such codes to be able to access their account more than once and to have reserve codes in case they made typos in some of the codes when writing them down.

The second requirement conflicts with the first one: short codes have low entropy, but for high security we need more entropy, so deciding on the length of codes is a balancing act between usability and security. Since our system is online, we can limit the number of attempts to enter codes, so the attacker can't perform the brute-force attack indefinitely. This is the rate limiting system discussed in the Rate limiting section: it is *required* for the system to be secure, so don't skip it.

For 2FA backup codes, given the limit of fifty guess attempts after which the account is locked, about 32 bits of entropy (that's more than 4 billion combinations) will be enough to be practically unguessable. To generate a code, use a secure random number generator, then encode the result into a readable format.

The encoding format is important for usability. I've seen many implementations of 2FA recovery codes that had awful formats: lowercase letters that are hard to distinguish from each other, a mix of lowercase and uppercase letters that will definitely be confused when typing from the piece of paper, etc. I would recommend either sticking with hex or numeric formats.

A 32-bit hex code looks like this:

```
e15b154e
```

It's a good idea to split characters into short groups to make them easier to write:

```
e15b-154e
```

Display the codes formatted as a list or a card so that it's easy to tell them apart, and use a monospaced font with a slashed or dotted zero:

- `a406-983c`

- `e7ef-2410`

- …

(Instead of circles for the list markers, consider empty squares that your users can mark to keep track of used codes.)

The hex encoding is easier to implement, but numeric Base10 codes are easier to write and read.

When implementing numeric codes, make sure not to introduce modulo bias (see Randomness section) — you can't simply do *mod 10* on each random byte.

An unsigned 32-bit number is a number from 0 to 4294967295, so the code will have 10 digits. The biggest 10-digit number is actually 9999999999, so you can fit a bit more entropy ($\log_2 9999999999$ ~= 33 bits) at the same code length. Why not?

If you have a *secure bias-free* string generator for which you can provide a custom alphabet, you can just generate a 10-character string containing digits from 0 to 9.

Some programming languages have secure random generators that can produce numbers in the required range. For example, in Python 3.6 and later:

```
>>> import secrets
>>> format(secrets.randbelow(10000000000), '09d')
'9869631473'
```

Do not use insecure random number generators! As discussed in the Randomness section, you should forget about them when implementing authentication.

Again, splitting the string into two parts would improve usability: instead of "9869631473", show the user two groups of five digits: "98696-31473".

Usually, ten to twelve codes are displayed to the user at once. After you generated the codes, store them on the server in the normalized form — without dashes or spaces. You should be able to show the codes in their formatted form to the user later, and allow the user to generate new codes, discarding the current ones.

To verify codes, normalize the code that the user entered (for hex codes, it's also a good idea to replace o's with zeros) — remove extra spaces and dashes — and then look it up in the stored list.

The user interface for your two-factor authentication should include a link to the form for entering the recovery key. Some apps allow entering the recovery code into the same input as the TOTP code. Since they have different formats (TOTP code has six digits, while the recovery code is longer), it's easy for the server to tell them apart. However, from the usability point of view, it seems not ideal since you can't force the correct formatting for the input field and the user might not realize that they should enter the recovery code, not the TOTP, which they don't have. I recommend using a different form.

—

[19] Quantum physicists will be in agony after reading this, but they deserve it for failing to properly explain their ways.

[20] https://twitter.com/mjos_crypto/status/1219423111826825217

[21] It's no longer collision resistant, but since TOTP doesn't rely on collision resistance, it is still okay for this purpose.

[22] https://tools.ietf.org/html/rfc6238

[23] CPCNSOASF means Computer People Can Never Settle On A Single Format. Just kidding, there's no such format. Yet.

Sessions

A session stores information about the logged in user so that they don't have to enter their password for each HTTP request. The safest sessions implementation uses a server-side database (which can be any SQL database, such as MySQL or PostgresSQL, a document database, such as MongoDB, or a key-value store, such as Redis) to store the identifying information, along with additional data, and uses client-side tokens that are sent by the client to the server in the HTTP request header (commonly, `Cookie` or `Authorization`) to look up the database record and perform user authentication.

There are no practical differences between web and mobile app sessions: both are using a server-issued session token to authenticate requests. The web app usually stores it in a cookie and provides it to the server automatically in the `Cookie` request header, while for mobile app, the session token is a *bearer* token which is usually provided to the server with each request in the `Authorization` or a custom header.

A secure session token should consist of two parts: an identifier and a verifier. For simplicity, they are concatenated into a single token. Upon receiving the token, the server splits it into the two values and performs verification.

When the user logs in, the server generates a random 16-byte identifier and a random 16-byte verifier. It records the identifier (as a primary key), the hash of the verifier, the expiration date, the user identifier and any extra information about the session in the database. It then concatenates and encodes the original 16-byte values (the identifier and the unhashed verifier) and sends them to the client to store and use for subsequent requests.

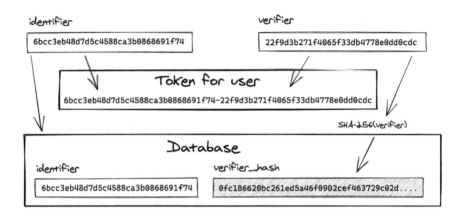

To authenticate the user, the server extracts the identifier and the verifier, searches the database for the identifier, and, if found, compares the hash of the verifier from the request with the hash stored in the database (using the constant-time comparison function as described in the Constant-time comparison section). If they are equal, the authentication succeeds.

Why do we need two values? Can't we just look up the record by the session identifier and be done? While it's true that it's infeasible to guess a 128-bit identifier (or a 122-bit one in case of UUID), the timing differences that the database has during the search may potentially be used to guess the correct session identifier byte-by-byte. This simple two-part construction prevents this since only the identifier is looked up by the value, but the verifier is compared in constant time.

Why hash the verifier? Consider an attacker who gets read-only access to the sessions database (for example, by compromising one of the backups you store in an S3 bucket that you accidentally made publicly accessible). By knowing the whole token, the attacker can just pretend to be the user. However, if you store the hash of the verifier, and give the original unhashed value to the user, the attacker can't construct the valid token because they don't know the original value and can't reverse a hash of the 128-bit value.

Note that the hash used here is a fast cryptographic hash, such as SHA-256, and not a password hashing function. If you want to save storage space, you can truncate the hash to 16 bytes, but I don't recommend it for simplicity reasons and to avoid mistakes, just use the whole 32-byte output of SHA-256.

The first value (or both, if you wish), can be UUIDv4, but make sure it is generated with a secure random byte generator. Unfortunately, there are many libraries for programming languages that generate UUIDs insecurely, which allows attackers to guess them. See the UUID section for details.

For MongoDB, ObjectId will work well as the session identifier, but not the verifier (ObjectId contains a 4-byte timestamp, a 5-byte random number and a 3-byte counter, which is not enough to make it unguessable).

Sessions have expiration dates after which they are no longer valid. The expiration date is a date relative to the last use of the session, not the session creation, since you don't want your users to be logged out periodically. Thus, the server should bump the expiration date each time the token is used. (To avoid excessive writing to the database, the server can compare only the date, not the whole time timestamp, and write the updated timestamp only if the date changes.) For most apps, the common practice is to expire a session after 30 days since its last use. Of course, banking or other high-risk apps should make sessions short-lived.

JWT and signed cookies for sessions?

Recently, JWT (JSON Web Token) and signed cookies became popular for identifying user sessions.

The idea is to have a single secret key known only to the server that is used to sign some user information, such as the user identifier, along with the expiration date. When the user presents this signed token, the server verifies the signature and checks the expiration date to authenticate the user. The advantage of this scheme is that it is stateless: the server doesn't need to keep any session state for users, it only needs to sign and verify tokens with a static key.

There is a huge weakness: tokens are valid until they expire. There is no real log out or a possibility to revoke other sessions before they expire.

Additionally, an attacker who gains one-time read-only access to the signing key can authenticate as any user until the leak is discovered and the key is rotated.

These weaknesses make this scheme completely unusable for anything other than toy projects.

The funny thing is that some developers try to fix the first problem by introducing a list of revoked tokens, which the server consults when validating tokens. Then they add bloom filters and other complications to make this list manageable. Basically, in addition to the authentication system, they build an anti-authentication system, failing to realize that by adding state they eliminate the only advantage of signed tokens, when they can just use a much simpler scheme!

Developers cite the improved scalability of JWT-based sessions due to the lack of state. But if their session storage (fewer than 64 bytes per entry retrieved in one cached database lookup) is a huge performance and scalability issue, what does their app do after the user is authenticated?

Sven Slootweg has a great flowchart called *Stop using JWT* for sessions. Take a look at it: http://cryto.net/~joepie91/blog/2016/06/19/stop-using-jwt-for-sessions-part-2-why-your-solution-doesnt-work/.

Don't use JWT or signed cookies for sessions.

In fact, I don't recommend using JWT for *anything*, even for short-lived tokens. It is a badly designed standard that leads to multiple vulnerabilities.[24] [25] [26]

Client-side session data

Ephemeral or temporary session data with short expiration period can be offloaded to the client that will store it in a cookie or the local storage. Note that there are size limits for both cookies and local storage in browsers.

Ephemeral session data must be signed (see Signed cookies) or encrypted (see Encrypted cookies), preferably with per-user keys stored in the sessions database.

However, remember the rule I mentioned earlier: if you can avoid cryptography, do avoid it. It's easier to use database or in-memory key-value storage for it.

Signed cookies

Signed cookies are sometimes useful when you want to offload storing pieces of state to the user's browser, making sure that when the server receives the cookie, it can verify that the user or an attacker didn't modify any information in it. Signed cookies cannot be revoked per-user, so don't use them for sessions or anything that needs revocation.

A signed cookie is a string that concatenates data with the signature. The signature is usually *symmetric*, what cryptographers call a *message authentication code* (MAC), since it doesn't use public-key cryptography. They are created and verified by a single message authentication function that takes a secret key and data and calculates a code (sometimes called a tag or an authenticator). When this operation is performed again on the same data, the function will return the same code. However, if the key or data changes, even by one bit, the code will change. An attacker won't be able to create a valid code without knowing the secret key, thus the secret key must be protected from leaking.

Usually, the message authentication function is HMAC (Hash-Based Message Authentication Code). HMAC takes a cryptographic hash function, a key, and data and returns a code of the same length as the output length of the hash. HMAC is commonly used with SHA-2 hash function family: SHA-256 or SHA-512. I recommend using HMAC-SHA-256, as it is widely available and works well on a wide variety of platforms. It returns a 32-byte code.

To create a signed cookie value, your server, which has a secret key, takes the value, computes an HMAC code, and then attaches this code to the original data.

To verify a signed cookie, the server splits the signed cookie value into the value and the code, computes the HMAC code from the secret key and the received value, and then compares the result with the received code in constant time. (Important! This comparison must be performed using a special comparison function that works in constant time. If you use the standard comparison function, it will be easy to break the system and generate valid signatures for your data without knowing the key! See the Constant-time comparison section for details.)

The simplest formatting for signed cookies is to separately encode the value and the signature using the Base64 URL-safe encoding, and then concatenate them with a separator character, such as ".". Here's an example of a signed cookie formatted this way:

```
aGVsbG8K.vyUqDaUAzgRg_6jU2CgrTeMjA8Ep91aSRHdbGsDdQX8=
```

If you split the string into two pieces, and then decode each part, you'll get the value "hello" and the randomly-looking 32-byte code.

Remember that the value is not encrypted! Everyone who has access to cookies can see what's inside, so don't put any sensitive information into it that you don't want to be seen. But nobody will be able to modify this cookie and make your server trust the modified value unless they know the secret key (or you have an implementation bug, of course).

A secret key for HMAC should contain 256 bits (32 bytes) of entropy from a secure random byte generator. Don't use smaller keys, and don't use passwords. Here's one way to generate a suitable key on Unix-like platforms:

```
$ head -c32 /dev/urandom > cookie_secret
```

This will write 32 bytes of randomness into the *cookie_secret* file. Alternatively, you can encode it in Base64:

```
$ head -c32 /dev/urandom | base64 # (or openssl base64 on
Linux)
```

To use it, decode it back from Base64. Alternatively, you can use the result directly for HMAC-SHA-256 without decoding it (the key will be a 44-character string containing 32 bytes of entropy).

If you use signed cookies in multiple places, use different keys for them — this will prevent confusion attacks when the attacker tries to use a value intended for one place in another place. Domain separation, as discussed in Prehashing for scrypt and bcrypt can also be used, but it's easier to use different keys.

Finally, make sure the secret key is kept safely on the server, you don't want it to leak. You should also periodically rotate the key — you may not know if the attacker gained access to your server or backups and stole the key.

Encrypted cookies

The reason to prefer encrypted cookies over signed cookies is that with encrypted cookies, the cookie value is kept secret from the user. However, signed cookies are easier to implement, so you're less likely to make mistakes.

Properly designed encrypted cookies use authenticated encryption, which provides confidentiality and authenticity. The authenticated encryption function adds a tag to the encrypted data, which works just like the code in signed cookies. When decrypting data, the function checks this tag to make sure the encrypted data was not modified. To create, encrypt, verify, and decrypt such cookies, the knowledge of the secret key is required.

Authenticated encryption is easy to get wrong: you will have to deal with *nonces* (sometimes called *initialization vectors*), cipher modes, and various parameters.

I recommend using XSalsa20-Poly1305 for authenticated encryption of cookies, as implemented in NaCl or Sodium libraries, with a randomly generated 24-byte nonce.

Alternatively, you can use AES-GCM or ChaCha20-Poly1305, which are available in most cryptographic libraries due to their inclusion in TLS, but you need to periodically rotate the encryption key since these authenticated encryption primitives have only 12-byte nonce: the more you use the same key with a random nonce, the more likely it is to collide, which will be catastrophic. You should not encrypt more than 2^{32} messages (cookie values or anything else) with the same key.

Periodic key rotation is a good idea anyway. To implement it, you can either prepend a key identifier to the ciphertext, and then use it to look up the key in the list, or just try to decrypt with the current key, and if it fails, try to decrypt with the previous key. In any case, don't store old keys for too long: remove them from the server after the expiration date.

If you use AES-GCM, make sure it is powered by the hardware AES CPU instruction, not a table-based implementation, which can be broken with timing attacks.

Definitely, do not use ECB, CBC, or any other mode. The exceptions are AES-SIV and AES-GCM-SIV, which are good, but unfortunately not widely available.

As I mentioned before, try not to use cryptography when it's not needed. Do not use signed or encrypted cookies — you can just store data on the server and reference it by the identifier stored in the cookie (see the Sessions section). Cryptography requires careful consideration and expensive audits. Getting it slightly wrong may lead to catastrophic results. You're less likely to screw things up by using the database.

Sessions list

When the user signs in on one device and then switches to another device and signs in there, the first session remains active: anyone who can use that first device is logged in. What happens if the user loses their device? What happens when they give the device to someone and forget to log out? The user needs to be able to see the devices they are signed in with and revoke access.

This is achieved by displaying the sessions list. You can see examples of such lists in Google's or GitHub's account preferences. The list contains all active sessions along with some additional information about them: the last time the session was used, the IP address and the geographic location where it was last used, the device or the browser name. There is also a button to revoke the session.

Sessions

By looking at this list, users can learn if their account was accessed by someone else and revoke sessions that they don't need anymore.

If you followed the advice on how to store sessions, creating and displaying such a list is just a matter of making a single database request. If you store the user agent in the database, you can format it to show the device name, such as "Safari on Mac" or "Firefox on Linux" (note that browser vendors intend to deprecate and remove the user agent string, so it may not work in the future). There are third-party packages, such as xojoc.pw/useragent for Go, that you can use to turn user agent strings into a readable text that you can display to the user.

You can also store and display a user's IP address that was last used with the session. You can turn it into a geographical location, so that your final list would display something like "Firefox on Linux at San Francisco, CA, USA". There are third-party packages to turn IP addresses into locations using a GeoIP database; a popular database is provided by MaxMind (https://www.maxmind.com).

User agents and IP addresses are not precise, so there may be some mistakes (for example, Belgium may become Netherlands or Firefox with a customized user agent string will show as Safari), but it is better than nothing. Note that the geographical location indicator may offend some users since international borders are disputed by many countries.

Revoking sessions

With the sessions design from this chapter, it is easy to revoke sessions. This operation is similar to logging out (see Logging out), but instead of deleting the record about the current session and clearing the cookie in the user's browser, the server deletes the session record requested by the user from the server's session storage. The next time the cookie for the revoked session is used, it simply won't be found in the database, so your app will ask the user to re-log in.

The sessions list displayed to the user should contain only the session identifier, not the verifier. The *Revoke session* button submits this identifier to the server. Since the session revocation endpoint requires the user to be authenticated, we do not care about the timing attack here. By not including the verifier, we ensure that it won't be possible to get all user's session tokens by looking at the list of sessions on just one device. (Of course, if you hashed the verifier on the server, as suggested, you don't even know the original verifier.)

Should you require the password for revoking a session? While it may protect against an attacker who takes temporary possession of the user's device and revokes all other sessions (which will only require the user to re-log in), it will also slow the user down if they discover that one of their devices has been stolen and they need to sign it out.

Logging out

Logging the user out is easy: just delete the current session record, the cookie, and redirect the user back to the log in form or the home screen. However, you need to make sure that logging out cannot be done via a cross-site request. If your app logged out users by visiting `https://example.com/logout` and stored session tokens in cookies, any website that puts

```
<img src="https://example.com/logout" />
```

on a page that the logged in user can visit would log them out.

The same applies if you use the POST request.

Make sure to use CSRF tokens everywhere you put the log out link.

If you want to have a separate page that the user can visit to log out, put a confirmation form protected with a CSRF token on it.

Since users can open your web app in multiple tabs or windows, all of them using the same session, you may need to communicate the fact that the user logged out in one tab to another, so that your app in another tab wouldn't try to perform actions in the unauthenticated state, getting errors from the server. You can use the JavaScript Broadcast Channel API (https://developer.mozilla.org/en-US/docs/Web/API/Broadcast_Channel_API) for this.

Server-side storage of sessions

If you have a single application server, store sessions in a database or a key-value store.

If you have many application servers, you can store sessions in a single shared database server. Alternatively, if you want each application server to have its own storage, you can use *sticky sessions*. Sticky sessions are sessions that are permanently assigned to a particular application server based on a cookie. When a request comes in, your load balancer reads the cookie and forwards it to the application server assigned to the cookie value. You can also shard sessions based on the session identifier: since it is random, the sessions will be partitioned uniformly.

Note that some databases (MySQL in particular, and PostgreSQL to a lesser extent) have reduced performance when the primary key is random, so you may want to stick four bytes of the current time in front of the identifier or replace the first four bytes of it with the timestamp. The performance reduction might not matter for your system, so just keep this possibility in mind, and stick with simple 16-byte random identifiers until you get real-world measurements. I'm sure that if this becomes an issue, you'll get more benefit from moving your sessions storage to Redis or something like it.

Client-side storage of session tokens

Web apps

The best place for web apps to store session tokens is cookies issued by the server. Make sure to set the following flags on the session cookie:

- `Secure` — to prevent sending the cookie over an unsecured HTTP connection.

- `HttpOnly` — to disallow reading the session cookie from JavaScript, protecting against cross-site scripting attacks that steal it.

- `SameSite` (`Strict`) — to enable protection against cross-site request forgery.

Don't forget to implement CSRF protection.

Storing session tokens using the client-side JavaScript code in cookies, local storage, or IndexedDB is not recommended since they can be stolen with a cross-site scripting attack.

Mobile apps

Mobile apps should store session tokens in the secure storage provided by the platform: Keychain on iOS or Keystore on Android. Make sure they are not accessible to other applications and not synchronized between devices.

—

[24] Critical vulnerabilities in JSON Web Token libraries, https://auth0.com/blog/critical-vulnerabilities-in-json-web-token-libraries/

[25] JWT: Signature-vs-MAC attacks, https://snikt.net/blog/2019/05/16/jwt-signature-vs-mac-attacks/

[26] JSON Web Token Validation Bypass in Auth0 Authentication API, https://insomniasec.com/blog/auth0-jwt-validation-bypass

Usability and accessibility

Registration form

In most early web apps registration forms were simple and fit in a single page. In today's world, this implementation simplicity isn't good enough for UI designers and marketing departments that try to improve sign up rates, so they split them into multiple screens. This may affect the security of users who use password managers.

A password manager is an app (or a web browser feature) that remembers passwords during the registration, stores them securely, and then fills the log in fields when the user opens the web app again. Password managers are vital for the security of users and help prevent phishing by autofilling passwords based on the web site URL.

Usually, password managers detect and save passwords when a form that contains input `type="password"` is submitted or when the browser navigates to another page (even if the navigation is emulated in JavaScript via `history.push`). If you split the form, make sure that you still have that field (even if it's hidden via CSS) in the actual form that is being submitted.

To improve usability, you may want to implement the password field that has an option to display the typed characters. Usually, this is implemented by replacing `type="password"` field with `type="text"` field when the user clicks on the "reveal" button. Make sure to convert the field back to the *password* type before submitting the form. Otherwise, some password managers may not be able to detect it and won't remember the password, frustrating the user.

The password field in the registration form should include `autocomplete="new-password"` attribute. Not all browsers recognize it yet, but in the future, this will help them decide which field they should autofill and remember. Browsers that don't recognize it will just ignore the attribute.

The username or the email address field should also include the autocomplete annotation, `autocomplete="username"` (or `autocomplete="username email"` when using email addresses instead of usernames).

Basically, your username field should look like this:

```
<input type="text" name="username"
autocomplete="username">
```

and your password field should look like this:

```
<input type="password" name="password" id="password"
autocomplete="new-password">
```

Do not use the `placeholder` attribute on inputs as labels: such inputs are hard to use for some people since the placeholder has a low contrast ratio and disappears when the user types text into the input. Use the proper `<label>` elements for those. (Some UI frameworks, such as Material UI for React, have accessible inputs: even though the label appears as a placeholder, it's actually implemented as a proper label element and doesn't disappear with typing; this solution is acceptable.)

It goes without saying, but unfortunately for some people it is not clear: do not try to prevent password managers from working with your web app. Your users will be more secure if they use one.

Sign in form

Sign in forms are simple: an input for the username or the email address and an input for the password. This is what we'll call a one-step sign in form. Some forms require the user to first enter their username or email address, click a button, and only then enter their password. This two-step process was created specifically for SAML authentication (which we won't discuss in this book) — if the user is registered with SAML authentication, after entering their username, they are redirected to their SAML provider to enter the password. Unfortunately, some developers saw this two-step process on their favorite web app and cargo-culted the implementation into their apps, which don't even use SAML. Even with the two-step form, it is important to make sure it works with password managers, otherwise, your users will use insecure passwords when they can't use their favorite password manager or will be very annoyed and switch to your competitors.

There are web sites that disable pasting of usernames or passwords and try to prevent users from using password managers. People who do this don't know what they are doing and should be ashamed of themselves — they make their users' security worse.

Test your forms with various password managers to make sure they work. Here are simple rules to follow:

- Use *username* or *email* as the name of the username input field and add `autocomplete="username"` attribute to it (when using email addresses, `autocomplete="username email"`).

- Use *password* as the name of the password input field and add `autocomplete="current-password"`.

- If you're using a two-step form, include the password field in the first step, hidden with CSS. Prefill the password field in the second step with the information from the first-step password field.

- If you're saving the username and displaying it as a text or a dropdown box, include a hidden read-only username field with the value identical to the displayed username.

For good accessibility, use `<label>` elements for input labels instead of abusing the `placeholder` attribute.

What about error handling? I've heard debates on whether the error that reports "incorrect username or password" is good for usability. Why don't we just say that the password is incorrect? There is an argument that it's to protect against guessing usernames, but in reality, this argument doesn't hold: you almost always can get this information by other means, such as simply trying to register an account with this username — the app will tell you that it's taken — or by trying to reset the password. No, the generic message is technically correct for a simple reason: while your server knows that the password is incorrect, it doesn't know whether the username is correct. If *johndoe* mistypes their username, entering *johndough*, and types the correct password for their *johndoe* account, and the actual user *johndough* exists, but, of course, has a different password, if you report "Incorrect password" error, this may confuse the user until they notice that the username is mistyped. You may, however, report that the user doesn't exist if there is no such user — this won't confuse anyone, and in fact, will help catch a mistyped username.

To summarize:

- "Username or password is incorrect" error should be used if the password is incorrect.

- "Username not found" error may be reported if the username doesn't exist.

However, if your app remembers the username and only requires entering the password, you can report "Incorrect password", since there can be no mistake in the username.

Afterword

Alright, now you know how to implement password authentication for web and mobile apps! Remember that even after reading this book cover to cover, you don't know *everything* about it. Nobody knows everything. I certainly don't.

Hopefully, it's enough to get you started on the right path and help you avoid common pitfalls. But you shouldn't stop learning or keeping up with infosec: as new vulnerabilities and attacks are discovered, you want to know about them to protect your app. Security is not something that you can think of from time to time — it's a process.

Be skeptical about everything you hear or read — there's a lot of bad advice out there. Think logically and systematically. Learn the basics of security. Learn a bit of cryptography (read *Serious Cryptography* by Jean-Philippe Aumasson), and try not to use it too much.

If your organization can afford to hire a security auditor, they should.

If you work for a bootstrapped startup or writing an open source app, ask for help from professionals, don't just copy and paste answers from StackOverflow.

Good luck!

About the author

Dmitry Chestnykh has been writing software for over twenty years. He consults on applied cryptography and software security. He was a member of the Password Hashing Competition experts panel. He discovered and helped fix numerous vulnerabilities in commercial and open source apps. You can find his code and documentation in Go and Python standard libraries. He wrote popular open source cryptography packages in JavaScript, Python, and Go.

Twitter: https://twitter.com/dchest

GitHub: https://github.com/dchest

Website: https://dchest.com

Index

www.ingramcontent.com/pod-product-compliance
Lightning Source LLC
LaVergne TN
LVHW041213050326
832903LV00021B/606